The Pocket Essential

MARILYN MONROE

Born Norma Jeane Mortenson in Los Angeles in the summer of 1926

Died Marilyn Monroe in Los Angeles in the summer of 1962

www.pocketessentials.com

First published in Great Britain 2000 by Pocket Essentials, 18 Coleswood Road, Harpenden, Herts, AL5 1EQ

Distributed in the USA by Trafalgar Square Publishing, PO Box 257, Howe Hill Road, North Pomfret, Vermont 05053

A CIP catalogue record for this book is available from the British Library.

ISBN 1-903047-31-5

9 8 7 6 5 4 3 2 1

Book typeset by Pdunk
Printed and bound by Cox & Wyman

For S.H.

Acknowledgements:

For their help, advice, encouragement, friendship and kindness, often above and beyond the call of duty, I would like to thank, in alphabetical order, the following: Steven Andrews, Richard Barkley, Jeremy Beadle, Mark Bego, Mo Bharwani, Peter Blackbrow, Vanessa Brannan, George Carpozi, Jr, David Castell, Jennifer Clarke, Patricia Denhard, Fletch Dhew, Virginia Dignam, Pat & Chris Dilworth, James Dougherty, John Du Pré, Diney & Stephen Dyer, Maria Edwards, James Elliott, Agnetha Fahlstrom, Philip French, Juliet Gaskell, Robin & Larry Goetz, Simon & Mark Gonzales, Kristian Green, Sarah Hall, Sharon Hall, the late Leslie Halliwell, Fiona Hammond, Jim Haspiel, Sharon Hawthorne, Sinéad Heffernan, Paul Hollingdale, Lesley Hughes, Tom Hutchinson, Angie Johnson, Laura Jones, Karen & Barry Kemelhor, the late John Kobal, Jo Knowsley & David Hensley, Phil Lawlor, Marion, Liz & Jim McHale, Dominic Midgley, Iwona Miloszewska, Bob Monkhouse, the late Eunice Murray, Brendan O'Mahony, Jenny Panton, Catherine Partridge, Sophie Payne, George Perry, the late Dilys Powell, Jayne Price, William Russell, Sue Sherman, the late David Shipman, Robert F. Slatzer, the late Milo Speriglio, James Steen, Rachel Stevens, Anthony Summers, Mitchell Symons, Wendy Taylor, Arthur Thirkell, Roy Turner, Shaun Usher, Alexander Walker, Ivan Waterman, Shannon Whirry, Monica & Mark White, Liz Williams and the late Maurice Zolotow.

CONTENTS

1. Introduction..7

A brief biography

2. Dumb: The Woo-Woo Girl.................................20

Early films from 1947 to 1951

3. Sexy: A Streetwalker Of Stunning Proportions...................33

Getting noticed in 1952

4.Fun: A Giggle In Her Talk.................................42

Starring roles from Niagara to The Seven Year Itch

5.Vulnerable: A Tenderness That Is Affecting...........................59

Taking her seriously, with Bus Stop, Some Like It Hot and The Misfits

6. Marilyn's Death...76

*Was she murdered? Did she commit suicide? Did she die accidentally?
Here are all the theories.*

7. The Best & Worst Films...................................78

A poll of leading film critics on both sides of the Atlantic

8. The 16 Directors Marilyn Agreed To Work With...................79

The chosen few

9. Where Are They Now?.....................................84

*What happened to some of the principals in Marilyn's life following
her death?*

10. Bibliography...93

The Monroe library

1. Introduction

"I want to be an artist and an actress with integrity. As I said once before, I don't care about the money, I just want to be wonderful."

"I never quite understood it – this sex symbol thing – I always thought cymbals were those things you clash together! That's the trouble, a sex symbol becomes a thing. I just hate to be a thing. But if I'm going to be a symbol of something I'd rather have it sex than some of the other things they've got symbols of."

For the past fifteen years or so the name of Marilyn Monroe has been linked more to the various conspiracy theories surrounding her death and less on her movie career. It is probably true to say that more books have been written about her than any other show-business celebrity. According to *The Guinness Book Of Film Facts & Feats*, she is the actress with the most biographies (Charlie Chaplin is the most written-about actor). Yet Marilyn has been dead for nearly forty years and her best films were made almost fifty years ago. But her image is still used by advertising agencies, record companies, movie studios, television companies and radio stations to promote their products. What is it about this woman that continues to fascinate and intrigue people who, like the present author, were not even born when Marilyn died?

Other women have been more beautiful. Other actresses have been more talented. Yet when we look back at the screen goddesses of the golden age of Hollywood, sure we remember Jean Harlow, Lana Turner, Rita Hayworth, Betty Grable, Joan Crawford and her great rival Bette Davis, Susan Hayward, Ann Sheridan et al, but it is Marilyn who stands head and shoulders above the rest. Ask almost any young person about the ladies mentioned above and, more often than not, you will probably be greeted with a blank stare but mention Marilyn Monroe and the recognition is instantaneous. Despite the often morbid preoccupation with her death, Marilyn Monroe remains the most potent sex symbol of the 20th century.

She began life in the Los Angeles General Hospital at 9.30am on Tuesday 1 June 1926. Her father is listed as Edward Mortenson, a 29-year-old baker from California, present whereabouts unknown. (Some believe that Mortenson was not Norma Jeane's real father and bolted when his wife became pregnant by one of her colleagues, Charles Stanley Gifford. In 1981 Mortenson died aged 83 in Riverside, California, from a heart attack.) Her Mexican-born mother, Gladys Pearl Monroe, had recently celebrated her 24th birthday and was working as a film cutter at Consolidated Film Industries. Insanity ran in Norma Jeane's family. Her great-grandfather, Tilford Hogan, would hang himself on 29 May 1933, at the age of 82. In July 1927 his daughter, Norma Jeane's grandmother, Della Mae Monroe Grainger attempted to smother the 13-month-old baby and was committed to Norwalk Metropolitan State Hospital. She died there on 23 August 1927. (Years later Marilyn Monroe would claim she could remember her grandmother trying to smother her. Although many authors have believed this impossible, her third husband, Arthur Miller, did indeed believe her.) On 20 November 1929, her 24-year-old uncle Marion Monroe told his wife he was going out to buy a newspaper and walked out on his family without explanation, never to return.

Gladys Baker (the surname of her first husband, Jasper, sometimes Jack, other times John Newton, Baker, and the one she used most frequently) decided to use her feminine wiles to ensnare a husband for herself and father for her latest offspring (she already had a son, Hermitt Jack (b. 24 January 1918 d. young), and a daughter, Berniece (b. 30 July 1919), by Jasper Baker). On 13 June 1926 she placed Norma Jeane with Albert Wayne and Ida Bolender, a religious couple, who lived at 459 East Rhode Island Street in Hawthorne, California. She paid them $5 a week to look after her daughter. Albert Wayne was a postman, a lanky, droop-shouldered man with a stern face. Ida was neat, if not fashionable, and her manner provided a pleasing contrast to that of her husband: she constantly wore a smile and her eyes twinkled behind horn-rimmed glasses. The Bolenders were religious fundamentalists or, by Gladys' standards, religious fanatics. Being a Christian Scientist she could not understand their negative attitudes nor their constant preaching on sin and hell. Meanwhile, Gladys went looking for a man believing a single woman would be more appealing than a single mother.

Gladys visited Norma Jeane every Saturday. The little girl stayed with the Bolenders until 1933 and then moved into another foster home for a brief period. On 20 October 1933 Gladys had saved enough money to put down a $750 deposit on a $6,000 bungalow at 6812 Arbol Drive, near the site of the Hollywood Bowl, and mother and daughter finally lived together. Among the skimpy furnishings was a white Franklin Baby Grand piano that once belonged to the actor Frederic March and a new wireless on which to listen to President Franklin D Roosevelt's Fireside Chats. Everything was bought on hire purchase but Gladys was confident that she could meet her commitments. She was working steadily at Columbia Pictures as a film cutter in the laboratory. It was monotonous work but it was reliable monotony that paid well. To make ends meet Gladys rented out the bungalow keeping two rooms for herself and Norma Jeane.

Another incident that has puzzled writers is Marilyn's claim that she was molested by one of the lodgers where she lived, a 'Mr Kimmell.' When she told her 'foster mother' what the 'star boarder' had done she was admonished for telling tales about such a fine man. It would seem likely that if the incident did happen, it happened at Arbol Drive for that is really the only place Norma Jeane ever lived that had lodgers. The 'star boarder' was the English actor Murray Kinnell. Marilyn may have slightly changed his name and invented the 'foster mother' to protect her own mother.

Gladys began to confide in one person – Grace McKee (b. Montana 1 January 1895 d. 6707 Odessa Drive, Van Nuys, 27 September 1953, a suicide. Buried at Westwood Memorial Park). Over the years, Grace, seven years older than Gladys, had become the kind of friend that one feels lucky to find once in a lifetime. More than once, when Gladys had found herself confused or unable to make a decision, Grace had intervened with the right solution. It had been Grace who had got Gladys a job at Columbia, who encouraged Gladys to buy Arbol Drive and to get Norma Jeane away from those religious fanatics. Gladys had long resolved that if anything happened to her, she wanted Grace to care for Norma Jeane. It can be said that Grace was Gladys' idol, perhaps even her alter ego. Grace was everything Gladys wanted to be.

Grace McKee had arrived in California in 1914, as Clara Grace Atchison, with aspirations of becoming a film star. Not long after her marriage to Reginald Evans, World War 1 left her a widow. Another marriage followed and by the time Gladys arrived on the scene, Grace had been promoted to foreman at Consolidated Film Industries. Grace was a small, trim woman whose dark blonde hair was usually dyed with peroxide. Grace was, to Gladys' eyes, chic. They had known each other for ten years and were aware of the other's idiosyncrasies. The only reason that they did not share Arbol Drive is because Gladys thought Grace 'a loose woman.'

The happiness did not last for, in January 1934, Gladys suffered a nervous breakdown and was taken to Los Angeles General Hospital (where Norma Jeane was born) for observation. She was later transferred to Norwalk (where her mother died) and declared a paranoid schizophrenic. On 15 January 1935, Gladys was declared mentally incompetent and her best friend Grace McKee was appointed Norma Jeane's legal guardian.

Grace McKee was a kind soul but she was also a practical one. For a while she and Norma Jeane lived with Grace's mother just off Hollywood Boulevard. On 10 August 1935, in Las Vegas, Grace married her divorced 6'5" beau Ervin Silliman 'Doc' Goddard, a wannabe inventor and Hollywood stand-in for Joel McCrea. A month later, on 13 September, Norma Jeane became the 3,463rd child sent to the Los Angeles Orphans' Home. Grace took Norma Jeane on outings usually to the cinema where she told the little girl that she, too, could become a big star. Grace encouraged Norma Jeane to try out her cosmetics and experiment with different hairstyles. Grace arranged for various foster families to look after Norma Jeane until she was able to provide a home herself. On 12 June 1937, eleven days after her eleventh birthday, Norma Jeane left the orphanage for the last time and moved in with Doc and Grace and his three children. Five months later, Norma Jeane was on the move again. Both Doc and Grace were heavy drinkers and one night Doc behaved inappropriately towards Norma Jeane. The girl moved in with her Aunt Olive (wife of the disappeared Marion) until August 1938 when she went to live with one of the most important people in her life 'Aunt' Ana Lower (b. 17 January 1880 d. 14 March 1948. Buried at Westwood Memorial Park).

Edith Ana Atchison Lower was a 58-year-old Christian Scientist and she was "the first person in the world I ever really loved. She was the only one who loved and understood me." In 1941 Norma Jeane moved back in with the Goddards until they announced they were moving to Huntingdon, West Virginia, where Doc had been transferred. They would not be taking Norma Jeane with them. In her usual practical way Grace decided the only thing to do was for Norma Jeane "to get married to the boy next door." Briefly, the girl returned to live with Ana Lower before her wedding to 21-year-old Jim Dougherty on 19 June 1942. Norma Jeane was given away by Ana Lower. At first the

10

marriage was a happy one - Jim Dougherty worked alongside Robert Mitchum and the future actor recalled how lovey-dovey the couple was. Dougherty told the present author that he and Norma Jeane had a very contented marital life. Cracks began to show, however, in late 1943 when the couple relocated to Catalina Island where he was a fitness instructor at the military base. Eventually, much to Norma Jeane's dismay, Dougherty applied for and received overseas duty. He sailed out of Catalina Island and out of the marriage.

In April 1944 Norma Jeane found work in the Radio Plane factory in Van Nuys, California. It was there she was discovered by army photographer David Conover who had been sent to take pictures of women helping the war effort by his commanding officer Captain Ronald Reagan. Conover's pictures caused a sensation and, on 2 August 1945, Norma Jeane went to see Emmeline Snively at the Blue Book Model Agency based in the Ambassador's Hotel, Los Angeles. (Bobby Kennedy would be shot dead in the same hotel 23 years later.)

Rechristened Jean Norman, the new model was a success. Norma Jeane's first magazine cover, for *Family Circle*, was published on 26 April 1946. On 26 June Conover shot her for *Yank* magazine. Emmeline Snively recommended her to Helen Ainsworth, an agent at the National Concert Artists' Corporation. It was Ainsworth who landed Norma Jeane her first interview with Ben Lyon at 20th Century-Fox on 17 July 1946. Lyon was impressed by what he saw and two days later arranged a colour screen test for Norma Jeane without getting the prior approval of his boss Darryl F Zanuck. The test went well and Norma Jeane was signed to Fox on 26 August 1946 at a fee of $75 per week. Lyon renamed her Marilyn Monroe after Marilyn Miller and Gladys' maiden name. On 13 September she was divorced from Jim Dougherty. (Grace Goddard helped Norma Jeane to get married and she helped Marilyn to get divorced. When Marilyn went to Nevada to establish residency for the divorce she stayed with Grace's Aunt Minnie.) The six-month contract was renewed for a similar period although her salary was doubled and Marilyn appeared in *Scudda Hoo! Scudda Hay!* (1948) and *Dangerous Years* (1947). However, the option on her contract was dropped on 25 August 1947 after she failed to make much impact in either film.

In February 1948 she was befriended by mogul Joseph M Schenck. He was born in Rybinsk, Russia, travelling to the States in 1892 and running errands for various shopkeepers until, with his brother Nicholas, he eventually owned a couple of New York chemists. They moved into the amusement arcade business in 1908 and opened their own amusement park four years later. They joined Marcus Loew in his chain of cinemas and the company that eventually became the parent of M-G-M. In 1917 Schenck branched out on his own and became an independent film producer. Seven years later in 1924 Schenck became chairman of United Artists and nine years after that co-founded 20th Century Pictures with Darryl F Zanuck. Two years later, he became chairman of the newly-formed 20th Century-Fox, a position he held until 1941. For a number of years Schenck had paid off two gangsters, Willie Biof and George Browne, to the tune of $50,000 *per annum*. The two had complete control of the stagehands' union and without their 'help' numerous productions would have been closed or run vastly over budget. The two men were eventually caught and jailed thanks in no small part to Schenck who served four months in prison for income tax evasion until he was pardoned by President Harry S Truman.

On 9 March Marilyn signed a contract with Columbia where she made just one film, *Ladies Of The Chorus*, before her option was dropped on 8 September. On New Year's Eve of that year she met the diminutive (5'3") but powerful agent Johnny Hyde who was to become her lover and mentor. On 27 May 1949, short of money, Marilyn posed nude for photographer Tom Kelley. She was paid a flat fee of $50. The pictures would become among the most celebrated photographs of all time. She returned to Fox to make three films: *A Ticket To Tomahawk* (1950), *The Fireball* (1950) and the one which gave her a second chance at Fox *All About Eve* (1950). Thanks to Hyde's influence Marilyn signed her new contract on 10 December 1950. Eight days later, Hyde died of a heart attack. Marilyn was beside herself with grief. Hyde had supposedly offered her $1million to marry him but she had refused because she was genuinely in love with him. She was asked by his family not to attend his funeral in deference to his sons but went anyway.

On 29 March 1951 Marilyn was a presenter at the Oscars, handing the statuette to Thomas Moulton for Best Sound Recording on *All About Eve*. Finally realising what they had on their hands, Fox signed Marilyn to a seven-year contract on 11 May 1951. It was worth $500 a week with semi-annual increases to a limit of $1,500. This was to cause Marilyn an awful lot of resentment in years to come and end with her going on strike. Marilyn then appeared in a succession of mostly unmemorable films but the public noticed her and her fan mail was enormous. In 1952 two momentous incidents occurred: the story of her nude calendar pose became public on 13 March; and she was cast as the unfaithful wife Rose Loomis in *Niagara* (1953), the film that was to make her a star.

Marilyn decided to throw herself on the public's mercy and tell the truth about the pictures. It was a successful strategy and the public did not turn against her as the studio feared. *Niagara* was the first film in which Marilyn's name appeared above the title. Behind the scenes, Fox was terrified over the sexual content of the story — impotence, adultery, honeymooners — and insisted it be toned down. The right-wing Daughters of the American Revolution campaigned against sex in the movies and were not happy at all with *Niagara*. *The Hollywood Daily Sketch* wrote: 'A film called *Niagara* in which Miss Monroe croons a song called *Kiss* has proved the last straw for the matrons. And they have made it clear to Miss Monroe's boss, Darryl F Zanuck, that Hollywood is in for another purity campaign unless something is done to curb the present spate of suggestiveness in films and publicity. Do their words carry any weight? The film company has postponed the release of a *Kiss* record by Marilyn Monroe.'

Marilyn's next assignment in November 1952 was co-starring with Jane Russell in *Gentlemen Prefer Blondes* (1953). Marilyn was a smash as Lorelei Lee beating out Fox glamour queen Betty Grable for the rôle. Marilyn showed she could act, sing and dance. Her rendition of *Diamonds Are A Girl's Best Friend* inspired Madonna and countless other artistes. Marilyn's next smash was the first comedy to be filmed in CinemaScope and teamed her with Grable and Lauren Bacall - *How To Marry A Millionaire* (1953) was the story of how three good-time girls set out to ensnare a rich husband. Most people expected there to be fireworks on set between Monroe and Grable – the upcoming glamour queen and yesterday's version. They were disappointed as the two women became firm friends. The film was released in November 1953 to critical acclaim.

Three months later, on 14 January 1954, Marilyn married baseball hero Joe DiMaggio in San Francisco's City Hall. At her new husband's insistence Marilyn dressed conservatively for the ceremony. Fred Guiles reported that Marilyn gave DiMaggio the explicit (showing pubic hair) pictures from the Tom Kelley nude session as a wedding present. On their honeymoon they visited Korea where Marilyn entertained the GIs stationed there. Marilyn was thrilled by the reception she received from the thousands of GIs telling DiMaggio she had never heard anything like it. DiMaggio, used to 70,000-plus sports fans screaming his name, quietly said: "Yes, I have." The marriage was not a happy one and was often punctuated by violence. DiMaggio had no patience for what he saw as Hollywood phoneys. That patience was stretched to the limit when Marilyn filmed the famous skirt blowing scene in *The Seven Year Itch* (1955) on 15 September 1954. He watched in stony silence as the crowd cheered every time his wife's dress was blown up by the tube train, then he stormed off. By October the marriage was over and Marilyn appeared alongside her lawyer Jerry Giesler to announce the separation. She was sporting a nasty bruise on her forehead caused by DiMaggio's fist.

That same year Marilyn appeared as saloon singer Kay Weston in *River Of No Return* (1954) opposite her first husband's ex-colleague Robert Mitchum, and as cloakroom attendant-turned-singer Vicky Parker in *There's No Business Like Showbusiness* (1954). Neither were great hits. On 31 December 1954, with the bisexual photographer Milton H Greene, Marilyn formed Marilyn Monroe Productions. Their aim was to produce motion pictures worthy of Marilyn's talent and to break the creative and financial stranglehold that Fox held over Marilyn. The studio retaliated by publicly threatening to sue her and privately by spinning against her playing the 'dumb blonde' card. Marilyn went on strike and a stand-off occurred until the summer of 1955 when *The Seven Year Itch* was released and gave Marilyn her first hit in two years. At the insistence of its shareholders Fox and Marilyn Monroe Productions began to negotiate a new contract. The new document signed a year to the day after the formation of her company gave Marilyn director and cinematographer approval, $100,000 per picture, the right to make just four pictures in seven years for the studio and $142,500 compensation.

On 3 May 1956 Marilyn began her first film under the new regime. It was the story of Cherie, a nightclub singer who longed to find a man to accept her for what she was, and a simple-minded cowboy on the lookout for a wife. Co-starring Don Murray, *Bus Stop* (1956) featured what is probably Marilyn's best performance. It was also the first film made under the guidance of Lee Strasberg, the proponent of Method acting, which has both baffled and helped many actors. It also coincided with her romance with playwright Arthur Miller - at the time Miller was under investigation by the House Un-American Activities Committee for his supposed left-wing views. The couple was married in a civil ceremony on 29 June 1956 and in a Jewish one 2 days later. The wedding was marred by the death in a car crash of 48-year-old journalist Princess Mara Scherbatoff of *Paris Match*. She was in a car trailing the Millers when her driver lost control and she was thrown through the windscreen. Arthur Miller tried to help but there was nothing anyone could do.

Marilyn was wont to combine her honeymoons with work and on this one she and Miller flew to England where she filmed Terence Rattigan's play *The Prince & The Showgirl* (1957) opposite Sir Laurence Olivier. Marilyn was to play Elsie Marina, the showgirl of the title. Olivier's wife, Vivien Leigh, had played the rôle on the London stage but was too old (at 42) for the screen version. Olivier stated that he had expected to fall in love with Marilyn during filming. He was to be disappointed. The leading man and lady did not gel off-screen. Olivier was exasperated by Marilyn's behaviour and her reliance on Paula Strasberg. However, despite their differences Olivier was to state later: "I was as good as could be; and Marilyn! Marilyn was quite wonderful, the best of all. So, what do you know?"

On 8 July 1958 Marilyn announced her next film was to be the Billy Wilder comedy *Some Like It Hot* (1959). The idea originated with *Fanfaren Der Liebe*, a musical in pre-Hitler 1932 Germany. Wilder was working for UFA and had seen the movie in which two musicians disguise themselves to fit into various scenarios: blacking up to play Negro music, wearing earrings and bandannas to play gypsy music, wearing drag to play in a girl band, etc. The original had overtones of sadism and lesbianism. Wilder altered the story to make it more palatable for movie audiences in America. It began filming on 4 August 1958 (four years to the day before Marilyn's death) and wrapped on 6 November 1958, twenty-nine days over schedule. It cost $2,800,000, having gone $500,000 over budget. Marilyn wanted the film to be shot in colour (as stipulated by her contract) but when the tests were shown, the made-up faces of co-stars Tony Curtis and Jack Lemmon looked distinctly green. She agreed to let Billy Wilder shoot in monochrome. Wilder hated colour films. He only shot his previous effort with Marilyn *The Seven Year Itch* in colour because of Monroe's contract. Filming at times was difficult because the leading lady was pregnant.

Marilyn took 47 takes to deliver the line "It's me, Sugar." She kept saying "It's Sugar, me" or "Sugar, it's me." Following the 30th take, Wilder had the line written on a blackboard. Another line also caused her problems. It was "Where's the bourbon?" The scene required Marilyn to search through a chest of drawers and deliver the line. Forty times she said either, "Where's the bottle?", "Where's the whisky?" or "Where's the bonbon?" Wilder had the line written on a piece of paper and put in the drawer. Then Marilyn became puzzled as to the location of the paper so Wilder placed it in every drawer. She took 59 takes to film the scene. Marilyn was not happy with her opening scene. Remembered Wilder, "She called me after the first daily rushes... I hung up and [screenwriter IAL] Diamond and I met and decided it was not good enough. She had just come on originally doing something with that ukulele. And we made up that new introduction with a new entrance [showing Sugar] coming down to the train through that puff of steam. She was absolutely right about that." Marilyn remembered it slightly differently: "I'm not going back into that fucking film until Wilder reshoots my opening. When Marilyn Monroe comes into a room, nobody's going to be looking at Tony Curtis playing Joan Crawford. They're going to be looking at Marilyn Monroe." (Marilyn's long-time friend, Jim Haspiel, remembers Marilyn only swearing once in front of him.) The film was a commercial and critical success reaching number three at the box office in 1959 earning $7,000,000 and a further $8,000,000 by 1964. Marilyn was paid $100,000 plus a 10% share of the gross profits. It was during this film that co-star Curtis made his notorious remark comparing kissing Marilyn to "kissing Hitler." She could not understand the comment. Her gay publicist, Rupert Allan, remembered Marilyn as saying to him, "That's a terrible thing to say about anybody. I don't understand it either because every morning he would stick in his head and say how beautiful I looked and how wonderful it was and how exciting." He later told *Time Out*, "She was a 600-pound gorilla, y'know. About 680 pounds actually... And she was like a mean 6-year-old girl. She would come and tell me that I was funnier than Jack Lemmon, and then she'd tell Jack she wished she were ending up with him at the end of the movie. It got to the point that nobody wanted to talk to her." Not long after filming wrapped Marilyn suffered a miscarriage.

On 1 October 1959 Marilyn began filming *Let's Make Love* (1960) opposite French actor Yves Montand. It was a prescient title - Marilyn and Montand had an affair under the noses of their respective spouses. Marilyn supposedly thought Montand would leave his wife Simone Signoret for her but the Gallic actor saw his dalliance as a mere fling. Perhaps the off-screen happenings affected Marilyn's performance because *Let's Make Love* is considered by some to be Marilyn's worst starring film.

During the filming of *Some Like It Hot* Arthur Miller had been turning his *Esquire* short story *The Misfits*, about a group of disaffected cowboys, into a vehicle for his wife. Marilyn's penultimate completed film was to be another fraught with difficulties despite co-starring with her childhood idol Clark Gable and her friend Montgomery Clift. Filming was delayed by the backlog caused by an actors' strike and finally began at 9am on 18 July 1960, but was shut down a week later because director John Huston's gambling caused a cash-flow problem. Marilyn's first scene was filmed on 21 July. Shooting was postponed on 30 July and again on 1 August because Marilyn was 'indisposed.' On 25 August filming shut down because Huston had bled the company financially dry. Marilyn took the opportunity to fly to Los Angeles for a long weekend. Huston had spoken to Marilyn's doctors Hyman Engelberg and Ralph Greenson and told them Marilyn, in his opinion, should be hospitalised for a week to rest. On 28 August Marilyn entered Westside Hospital in Los Angeles. Producer Frank Taylor announced Marilyn had suffered 'a breakdown' and filming would be suspended for a week. It gave Huston time to find new finance. On 5 September Marilyn returned to Reno but was ill again on 12, 13 and 19 September. Studio filming began on 24 October with Marilyn and Eli Wallach in a scene involving a truck. The film wrapped on 4 November 1960. It had cost $3,955,000 — the most expensive black and white film then made — and gone 40 days over schedule.

Marilyn's marriage to Arthur Miller fell apart and the crew of *The Misfits* divided into two camps. Marilyn found Miller's diary where he had written a less than complimentary entry about her. "I'm not just a dumb blonde this time, I'm a crazy dumb blonde. And to think, Arthur did this to me. He was supposed to be writing this for me. He could have written anything and he came up with this." They flew home to New York from Hollywood in separate aeroplanes. On Friday 11 November a week after the film wrapped the couple announced they would divorce. Five days later, Clark Gable died after suffering a massive heart attack. The press jumped on Marilyn, claiming her behaviour on the set caused Gable's death. No one mentioned that 59-year-old Gable insisted on doing all his own stunts, and that he smoked 60 cigarettes a day for over 30 years. When the film premièred on 31 January 1961 critics were not kind. Bosley Crowther of *The New York Times* wrote 'It has something to do with freedom. What, we couldn't know… So that's what's wrong with this picture. Characters and theme do not congeal. There is a lot of absorbing detail in it, but it doesn't add up to a point. Mr Huston's direction is dynamic, inventive and colourful. Mr Gable is ironically vital. (He died just a few weeks after shooting was done.)…But the picture just doesn't come off.'

Marilyn and Arthur Miller were divorced on 20 January 1961, a day chosen to lessen press coverage because it coincided with the inauguration of America's first Roman Catholic President John F Kennedy. Marilyn spent much of 1961 hospitalised for various physical and mental ailments. On 23 April 1962 she began filming *Something's Got To Give* opposite Dean Martin. The film was directed by George Cukor who had previously worked with Marilyn on *Let's Make Love*. At the same time Elizabeth Taylor was in Rome filming the epic *Cleopatra* (1963), the movie which eventually bankrupted 20th Century-Fox. It seemed as if the studio wanted Marilyn to leave her film so they could sue her for $1 million for breach of contract and recoup some of the money laid out on *Cleopatra*. The script was regularly changed and the new pages were only sent to Marilyn at the last moment.

Marilyn was invited to sing *Happy Birthday* to President Kennedy at his Madison Square Garden birthday party on 19 May 1962 but the studio publicly forbade her to go. Privately, a memo was issued granting permission. Producer Henry Weinstein today admits that if he had been more experienced he would have made a press and publicity junket out of the trip to gain even more exposure for the film. Feigning a cold, she flew to New York anyway where the MC Peter Lawford introduced her as "the late Marilyn Monroe," a gentle dig at her constant tardiness. In fact, Lawford had been introducing Marilyn regularly throughout the evening and each time she failed to appear it was as part of a running gag. She wasn't due to appear until the very end of the gala. Marilyn was escorted by Isidore Miller, her former father-in-law, but rumours have surfaced over the years that she spent the night with the President at the Carlyle Hotel and may even have taken part in an orgy that night. Marilyn's friend Jim Haspiel, who attended the event, disputes this. "I can tell you with *authority*, that I was with Marilyn at her apartment at ten minutes to four in the morning. Categorically, Marilyn was not asleep at the Carlyle Hotel, and I didn't notice the President anywhere nearby us, either!"

Nine days after the Madison Square party, Marilyn filmed the famous nude swimming scene for *Something's Got To Give* - she was not a good swimmer utilising an unusual doggy paddle. She celebrated her 36th birthday. On 4 June she was bedridden with a temperature over 100 degrees. Four days later, she was fired. An advertisement was placed in *Weekly Variety*, supposedly by the crew, 'thanking' Marilyn for losing them their jobs. It was actually placed by executives of 20th Century-Fox, once again spinning against their biggest female star. Negotiations begun in earnest. Dean Martin refused to appear with anyone else. Marilyn was offered $500,000 for the film plus a bonus if it was completed on time. The film was due to reshoot from 16 September. It was not to be…

2. Dumb: The Woo-Woo Girl

Dangerous Years
(20th Century-Fox, 7 December 1947)

The Crew: Director Arthur Pierson. Writer Arnold Belgard. Producers Sol Wurtzel & Howard Sheehan. Cinematographer Benjamin H Kline. Editor Frank Baldridge. Music Rudy Schrager. Art Director Walter Koessler. Editing Assistant William F Claxton.

The Cast: William Halop (Danny Jones), Ann E Todd (Doris Martin), Jerome Cowan (Weston), Anabel Shaw (Connie Burns), Richard Gaines (District Attorney Edgar Burns), Scotty Beckett (Willy Miller), Darryl Hickman (Leo Emerson), Harry Shannon (Judge Raymond), Dickie Moore (Gene Spooner), Donald Curtis (Jeff Carter), Marilyn Monroe (Eve), 62 minutes.

The Story: A look at juvenile delinquency in the 1940s. Danny (former Dead End Kid Billy Halop) prevents other youngsters from enjoying the facilities of a boys' club and goes on to arrange a robbery. Marilyn plays a waitress at the Gopher Hole, a café where they spend their time.

Behind The Scenes: Marilyn shot the film in the summer of 1947. Her contract was dropped on 25 August 1947, four months before its release.

Did You Know?: This contains Marilyn's first speaking rôle on screen. Although made after *Scudda Hoo! Scudda Hay!* It was released first. The film flopped when it was released with many newspapers, including the prestigious *New York Times*, failing even to review it.

What The Critics Say: 'Some of the causes of juvenile delinquency, and some of the adult policies designed to offset them, are explored interestingly here in a melodrama forcefully directed by Arthur Pierson' William A Weaver, *Motion Picture Herald*.

Scudda Hoo! Scudda Hay!
(20th Century-Fox, 14 April 1948)

The Crew: Director & Writer F Hugh Herbert. Story George Agnew Chamberlain. Producer Walter Morosco. Cinematographer Ernest Palmer. Editor Harmon Jones. Music Cyril J Mockridge. Music Conductor Lionel Newman. Art Direction Albert Hogsett & Lyle R Wheeler. Set Decorator Stanley Detlie. Wardrobe Charles LeMaire. Costumes Bonnie Cashin. Orchestration Earle Hagen & Herbert Spencer. Make-Up Ben Nye. Special Photographic Effects Fred Sersen. Sound Eugene Grossman & Roger Herman, Sr.

The Cast: June Haver (Rad McGill), Lon McCallister (Snug Dominy), Walter Brennan (Tony Maule), Anne Revere (Judith Dominy), Natalie Wood (Bean McGill), Robert Karnes (Stretch Dominy), Henry Hull (Milt Dominy), Tom Tully (Roarer McGill), Les MacGregor (Ches), Geraldine Wall (Mrs McGill), Marilyn Monroe (Girl In Rowing Boat), 95 minutes.

The Story: Snug Dominy buys two mules and then is torn between advice he receives from various people. Yawn.

Did You Know?: The film is also known as *Summer Lightning*. Marilyn had one line, actually one word, "Hello," which was cut prior to the film's release.

What The Critics Say: 'The objects of paternal admiration in this film are, of all things, a pair of mules. At least, they're the major interest of Fox's perennial farm boy, Lon McAllister, in this rural romance... To the average person, however, it is questionable whether these mules will have quite the same fascination as previous beasts seen on Fox's model farm' Bosley Crowther, *The New York Times*.

Ladies Of The Chorus
(Columbia, 22 October 1948)

The Crew: Director Phil Karlson. Writers Joseph Carole & Harry Sauber. Story Harry Sauber. Producer Harry A Romm. Cinematographer Frank Redman. Editor Richard Fantl. Music Mischa Bakaleinikoff. Art Direction Robert Peterson. Set Decoration James A Crowe. Production Number Stager Jack Boyle.

The Cast: Adele Jergens (May Martin), Marilyn Monroe (Peggy Martin), Rand Brooks (Randy Carroll), Nana Bryant (Mrs Adele Carroll), Eddie Garr (Billy Mackay), Steven Geray (Salisbury, Carroll's butler), Bill Edwards (Alan Wakely), Marjorie Hoshelle (Bubbles LaRue), Frank J Scannell (Joe, the stage manager), Dave Barry (Ripple, the decorator), 61 minutes.

The Story: Burlesque singer Peggy Martin is the daughter of another burlesque queen. However, when Peggy is romanced by socialite Randy Carroll her mother is worried that the social gap between them may be too great a distance for love to bridge. Her fears seem to be realised at the lovers' engagement party when Peggy is humiliated but the couple manage to put their social differences behind them and love conquers all.

Behind The Scenes: Marilyn was wooed by her divorced vocal coach Freddy Karger (1916-1979) during her time at Columbia. It was Karger whom Marilyn referred to as her first real love. He taught her about fine food and good music. He also arranged for her to have her teeth corrected. She often stayed with his mother, Anne known as 'Nana.' When Marilyn wanted to marry Karger he let her down cruelly. She had bought – on tick – a $500 watch for him and was still paying for the gift long after the end of the relationship. He later went on to marry, divorce, remarry and redivorce actress Jane Wyman. It was also during this period that she began working with drama coach Natasha Lytess (1903-1964).

Did You Know?: This low budget musical was Marilyn's first co-starring film. Marilyn said: "I kept driving past the theatre with my name on the marquee. Was I excited. I wished they were using 'Norma Jeane' so that all the kids at the home and schools who never noticed me could see it." Despite being under contract to the studio for six months, *Ladies Of The Chorus* was Marilyn's only film for Columbia. Studio chief Harry Cohn was unimpressed by her. Adele Jergens played Marilyn's mother even though she was only eight years and seven months older.

What The Critics Say: 'Miss Monroe is cute and properly naïve' *Hollywood Reporter*. 'Enough musical numbers are inserted, topped with the nifty warbling of Marilyn Monroe… Miss Monroe presents a nice personality in her portrayal of the burley singer' *Variety*. 'One of the bright spots is Miss Monroe's singing. She is pretty and, with her pleasing voice and style, she shows promise' Tibor Krekes, *Motion Picture Herald*.

The Verdict: A surprisingly good film. 2/5

Love Happy
(United Artists, 8 April 1950)

The Crew: Director David Miller. Writers Mac Benoff & Frank Tashlin & Ben Hecht. Story Harpo Marx. Producers Lester Cowan & Mary Pickford. Cinematographer William C Mellor. Editors Albrecht Joseph & Basil Wrangell. Music Ann Bonnell. Musical Direction Paul J Smith. Orchestration Harry Geller. Make-Up Fred B Phillips. Hairstyles Scotty Rackin. Production Designer Gabriel Scognamillo. Photographic Effects Howard A Anderson. Production Number Stager Billy Daniel. Production Manager Ray Heinze. Set Decoration Casey Roberts.

The Cast: Harpo Marx (Harpo), Chico Marx (Faustino), Groucho Marx (Sam Grunion), Ilona Massey (Madame Egelichi), Vera-Ellen (Maggie Phillips), Marion Hutton (Bunny Dolan), Raymond Burr (Alphonse Zoto), Melville Cooper (Lefty Throckmorton), Paul Valentine (Mike Johnson), Leon Belasco (Mr Lyons), Marilyn Monroe (Grunion's Client), 85 minutes.

The Story: Detective Sam Grunion relates how he uncovered the Romanoff diamond theft. A troupe of poor actors try to smuggle the jewels into America inside a tin of sardines. Marilyn plays a client of Grunion's but apart from looking gorgeous she has nothing really to do with the plot.

Behind The Scenes: Marilyn had been unemployed for almost six months when she was cast in a bit part in *Love Happy*. Marilyn auditioned for Groucho who told her she had "the prettiest ass in the business." In June 1949 Marilyn went on a promotional tour for the film and stopped off in New York. She believed New York was much chillier than Los Angeles and so packed only warm clothes. She arrived in the middle of a heatwave. She was pictured in several newspapers sweating in her clothes cooling off with ice creams. The press nick-named her 'The Woo Woo Girl' and 'The Mmmm Girl.'

Did You Know?: *Love Happy* was the last Marx Brothers film. It was a flop. Despite this being her fourth film her screen credit reads 'Introducing Marilyn Monroe.' This film was the first cinematic instance of Marilyn's wiggle, later seen to better effect in *Niagara*. Marilyn was paid $500 plus another $300 for promotional photographs and $100 a week for the tour.

What The Critics Say: 'Harpo's brilliant gift for pantomime gets free play as Chico reads his mind and the musical accompaniments of Harpo at the harp, natch, and Chico at the piano provide a pleasant con-trast to their energetic clowning. The Marx Brothers are in fine fettle and, as seems to be the case in recent years, they appear to be much better than their material' TMP, *The New York Times*.

The Verdict: Marilyn looking terrific is enough to earn 1/5

A Ticket To Tomahawk
(20th Century-Fox, 19 May 1950)

The Crew: Director Richard Sale. Writers Mary Loos & Richard Sale. Producer Robert Bassler. Cinematographer Harry Jackson. Editor Harmon Jones. Music Cyril J Mockridge. Art Direction George W Davis & Lyle R Wheeler.

The Cast: Dan Dailey (Johnny Behind-the-Deuces), Anne Baxter (Kit Dodge, Jr), Rory Calhoun (Dakota), Walter Brennan (Terence Sweeny), Charles Kemper (Chuckity), Connie Gilchrist (Madame Adelaide), Arthur Hunnicutt (Sad Eyes), Will Wright (Dodge), Chief Yowlachie (Pawnee), Mauritz Hugo (Dawson), Marilyn Mon-roe (Clara), Jack Elam (Fargo), 90 minutes.

The Story: 1876: Dawson runs a stagecoach but is worried that if the new-fangled steam train starts running his business will go bankrupt. With this in mind he hires a gunslinger called Dakota to stop the train taking the strain.

Behind The Scenes: Marilyn auditioned for the rôle of Clara on the advice of lover-mentor Johnny Hyde. It was her first film at Fox since her contract was not renewed two years earlier. However, the film did nothing for her career.

Did You Know?: The film took 5 weeks to shoot in Durango, Colo-rado. The costume worn by Marilyn was the first specifically designed for her by 20th Century-Fox. The film suffered because of poor reviews of the Betty Grable *flick The Beautiful Blonde From Bashful*

Bend, and so Fox were unwilling to spend too much on marketing and promotion fearing another Western flop.

What The Critics Say: 'By George, it's a pretty good show... There's a lot of pleasure in *A Ticket To Tomahawk*. Viewed as an uncompetitive venture (to *Annie Get Your Gun*), it offers surprising good fun... filmed, for the most part, amid scenery that is lovely on the Technicolored screen. Shot very largely on location in western Colorado, it does have an airiness and a beauty that you don't often find in such films. Likewise, the outdoor action of transporting a real old-fashioned iron horse, first by track and then by mule train, has flavour and humorous gusto' Bosley Crowther, *The New York Times*.

The Verdict: Not bad at all. 2/5

The Asphalt Jungle
(M-G-M, 23 May 1950)

The Crew: Director John Huston. Writers Ben Maddow & John Huston. Novel W R Burnett. Producer Arthur Hornblow, Jr. Cinematographer Harold Rosson, ASC. Art Directors Cedric Gibbons & Randall Duell. Editor George Boemler. Music Mikos Rosza. Sound Douglas Shearer. Set Decoration Edwin B Willis & Jack D Moore. Hairstyles Sydney Guilaroff. Make-Up Jack Dawn.

The Cast: Sterling Hayden (Dix Handley), Louis Calhern (Alonzo D Emmerich), Jean Hagen (Doll Conovan), James Whitmore (Gus Minissi), Sam Jaffe (Doc Erwin Riedenschneider), John McIntire (Police Commissioner Hardy), Marc Lawrence ('Cobby' Cobb), Barry Kelley (Lieutenant Ditrich), Anthony Caruso (Louis Ciavelli), Teresa Celli (Maria Ciavelli), Marilyn Monroe (Angela Phinlay), Strother Martin (Karl Anton Smith), 112 minutes.

The Story: Corrupt copper Lieutenant Ditrich is called into the Commissioner's office for a dressing down over his failure to halt the crime wave that has been occurring. He is given one last chance to clean up the city. Meanwhile, just out of pokey, Doc Erwin Riedenschneider goes to 4717 Camden West to visit criminal go-between and bookie 'Cobby' Cobb with a plan to rob the jewellers, Bellateers. He reckons it will net them a cool $500,000 but needs $50,000 up front to finance the heist. He wants Cobby to approach bent lawyer Alonzo D Emmerich but the legal eagle has a problem - he's broke. Gus Minissi is the hunchbacked owner of the local café and something of a father figure to the alcoholic, cerebrally-challenged 'hooligan' Dix Handley. He loans him $2,500 so he can pay his debt to Cobby. Dix also has woman trouble. The lovely Doll turns up and asks if she can stay a day or two – her residence, a clip joint, has been raided and on pay day of all days. He likes her but – typical bloke – doesn't want a commitment. Despite being broke Emmerich is intrigued by Doc's plan and sets the wheels in motion. He is owed $100,000 by various clients but despite the best efforts of his own private dick, Bob Brannom, none of them pay up. They cook up a plan to keep all the profits from the heist for themselves. Brannom persuades the gullible Cobby to stump up the $50K and they hire their 'boxman' (safe cracker) for $25,000, driver for $10,000 and the muscle or 'hooligan' for $15,000. During the robbery burglar alarms begin going off for no reason, the drill bit breaks and the boxman Louis Ciavelli is accidentally shot in the stomach. Back at Emmerich's, he and Brannom wait for their booty. When Doc and Dix return they suspect a double-cross and in a brief gun battle Dix shoots and kills Brannom but is shot himself. Doc offers Emmerich a way out of his predicament – contact the jeweller's insurance company and arrange a buy-back for $250,000 no questions asked. As they leave Doc and Dix bump into a special constable and before Dix can knock him out Doc gets a nasty gash to his head. Meanwhile, Emmerich's mistress, Angela, gives him a false alibi for the time of the heist. Ditrich goes to see Cobby to urge him to turn state's evidence. For her safety Emmerich decides to send Angela away but as they are planning her trip to Cuba the police arrive to arrest him for complicity in robbery and murder. Before the arrest can be made, Emmerich takes his own life although the viewer sees neither the gun nor the firing of the weapon. Back at Doll's house Dix and Doc go their separate ways. She offers to drive Dix home to Kentucky while Doc finds a German taxi driver and gives him a $50 tip to drive him to Cleveland. Doc's passion for beautiful young girls is his downfall and Dix just about makes it to Hickory Wood Farm before he, too, gives up the ghost.

Behind The Scenes: There are various theories as to how Marilyn landed the part of Angela Phinlay. One has it that her then agent and lover Johnny Hyde pulled all sorts of strings. Another has it that she turned up to an audition with a padded bra and director Huston removed the falsies and told her she had the part. A third has Huston keeping horses at a ranch belonging to Lucille Ryman and John Carroll. He had fallen behind with his payments to the tune of $18,000 and the pair 'insisted' Huston cast Marilyn or they would sell his beloved horses. Huston's first choice for Angela was the blonde Lola Albright but she was too expensive. He then screen tested eight others before testing Marilyn. Marilyn's drama coach Natasha Lytess stood in Marilyn's line of vision during her scenes and nodded her approval or otherwise. If you watch carefully in Marilyn's last scene you can see her looking at Lytess as she walks off set.

Did You Know?: M-G-M supremo Louis B Mayer hated the film. He said "That Asphalt pavement thing is full of nasty, ugly people doing nasty things. I would walk across a room to see a thing like that." When the film premièred one of the policemen on duty to keep the crowds at bay was Jim Dougherty, Marilyn's first husband. Marilyn regarded the film as one of her best performances: "I don't know what I did but I do know it felt wonderful." The film was nominated for four Oscars – Best Cinematography, Best Director, Best Screenplay and Best Supporting Actor – but failed to pick up any of the prizes.

What The Critics Say: 'The players under Mr Huston's guidance carry out their assignments with unmistakable skill. The rôles are unsympathetic but they are played with ability... Less attention is given to the feminine characters. Among them are Jean Hagen as a sketchily drawn nightclub girl infatuated with the gunman. Marilyn Monroe as a young woman on whom the lawyer lavishes his money, and Dorothy Tree as his neglected wife' – EFM *in Christian Science Monitor*. 'This brutally frank story of crime and punishment in a Midwestern city... packed with stand-out performances... There's a beautiful blonde, too, name of Marilyn Monroe, who plays Calhern's girlfriend, and makes the most of her footage' – Liza Wilson in *Photoplay*.

The Verdict: The film still has its moments although it does, at times, appear corny in the extreme. Some of the performances seem a little over the top but Sam Jaffe is believable as the criminal mastermind and Monroe shines in her brief rôle. She shows the definite makings of a star. 3/5

All About Eve
(20th Century-Fox, 14 October 1950)

The Crew: Director Joseph L Mankiewicz. Writers Joseph L Mankiewicz & Mary Orr. Story *The Wisdom Of Eve* Orr. Producer Darryl F Zanuck. Cinematographer Milton R Krasner. Editor Barbara McLean. Music Franz Liszt & Alfred Newman. Production Designers George W Davis & Lyle R Wheeler. Art Direction Lyle R Wheeler. Set Decoration Walter M Scott. Wardrobe Direction Charles LeMaire. Costumes Edith Head & Charles LeMaire. Assistant Director Gaston Glass. Orchestration Edward B Powell. Make-Up Ben Nye. Special Photographic Effects Fred Sersen. Sound WD Flick & Roger Heman. German Dialogue Coach Erich Kästner.

The Cast: Bette Davis (Margo Channing), Anne Baxter (Eve Harrington), George Sanders (Addison De Witt), Celeste Holm (Karen Richards), Gary Merrill

(Bill Sampson), Hugh Marlowe (Lloyd Richards), Gregory Ratoff (Max Fabian), Barbara Bates (Phoebe), Marilyn Monroe (Claudia Caswell), Thelma Ritter (Birdie), 138 minutes.

The Story: Eve Harrington is a talented actress who wants to make it to the top on Broadway. She seizes her opportunity when she is hired as a secretary to *grande dame* Margo Channing. Eve uses Margo's friends and contacts to push herself. She becomes Margo's understudy and with the help of Karen, Margo's mate, Eve takes to the stage when Margo is unable to get to the theatre. A star is born and Eve then makes a play for Margo's boyfriend but he is having none of it. She then tries to blackmail Karen into letting her star in Karen's husband's next play. Margo pulls out of the play to marry her boyfriend and Eve gets another chance. Then a young actress called Phoebe comes on the scene…

Behind The Scenes: Once again it was Johnny Hyde who worked to get Marilyn cast in this film. In March 1950 he introduced Marilyn to director Joseph L Mankiewicz and on the 27th of the month she was signed to $500 a week. In fact, she was so good in the few scenes she appeared in that Darryl F Zanuck offered her another contract that kicked in when she made *As Young As You Feel*, despite his personal animus towards her.

Did You Know?: When Marilyn's writer friend Sidney Skolsky wanted to page her without drawing too much attention he would use the name 'Miss Caswell,' her character in *All About Eve*. Set decorator Walter M Scott won the first of his 22 Oscar nominations for his work on *All About Eve*. The film's working title was *Best Performance*. The film was nominated for 11 Oscars winning 6.

What The Critics Say: 'In *All About Eve*… a withering satire – witty, mature and worldly-wise, which 20th Century-Fox and Joseph Mankiewicz delivered to the Roxy yesterday, the movies are letting Broadway have it with claws out and no holds barred. If Thespis doesn't want to take a beating, he'd better yell for George Kaufman and Moss Hart. As a matter of fact, Mr Kaufman and Mr Hart might even find themselves outclassed by the dazzling and devastating mockery that is brilliantly packed into this film. For obviously, Mr Mankiewicz, who wrote and directed it, had been sharpening his wits and talents a long, long time ago for just this go. Obviously, he had been observing the theatre and its charming folks for years with something less than an idolater's rosy illusions and zeal. And now, with the excellent assistance of Bette Davis and a truly sterling cast, he is wading into the theatre's middle with all claws slashing and settling a lot of scores' Bosley Crowther, *The New York Times*.

The Verdict: A stunning film. 3/5

The Fireball
(Thor/20th Century-Fox, 9 November 1950)

The Crew: Director Tay Garnett. Writers Tay Garnett & Horace McCoy. Producer Bert E Friedlob. Cinematographer Lester White. Editor Frank Sullivan. Music Victor Young.

The Cast: Mickey Rooney (Johnny Casar), Pat O'Brien (Father O'Hara), Beverly Tyler (Mary Reeves), Glenn Corbett (Mack Miller), James Brown (Allen), Marilyn Monroe (Polly), Ralph Dumke (Bruno Crystal), Bert Begley (Shilling), Milburn Stone (Jeff Davis), Tom Flint (Dr Barton), 84 minutes.

The Story: Orphan Johnny Casar runs away and lands a job as a professional roller skater. Thanks to his dedication he succeeds, but after a while the success goes to his head. He stops being a team player and thinks only of himself. He takes up with wild girls like Polly, something of a skating groupie. When he comes down with a bout of polio, it is his old friend Mary who looks after him.

Behind The Scenes: Marilyn wasn't keen to make the film and Johnny Hyde had to spend a quarter of an hour talking her round.

Did You Know?: The film is also known as *The Challenge*.

What The Critics Say: '*The Fireball* has a few good moments in the skating sequences, in Pat O'Brien's droll portrayal of the priest, and, paradoxically, during the early scenes of Mr Rooney's vagrancy' HHT in *The New York Times*.

The Verdict: Another film in which Marilyn sparkles but has yet to shine. 2/5

Right Cross
(M-G-M, 15 November 1950)

The Crew: Director John Sturges. Writer Charles Schnee. Producer Armand Deutsch. Cinematographer Norbert Brodine. Music David Raksin. Art Direction Cedric Gibbons & James Scognamillo.

The Cast: June Allyson (Pat O'Malley), Dick Powell (Rick Garvey), Ricardo Montalban (Johnny Monterez), Lionel Barrymore (Sean O'Malley), Barry Kelley (Allan Goff), Teresa Celli (Marina Monterez), Mimi Aguglia (Mom Monterez), Marianne Stewart (Audrey), John Gallaudet (Phil Tripp), Kenneth Tobey (Journalist), Marilyn Monroe (Dusky Ledoux), 90 minutes.

The Story: Champion boxer Johnny Monterez suffers racist abuse because he's Mexican. He falls in love with his trainer's daughter, Pat. Johnny turns down a big fight because of his love for Pat. His best friend is the sports journalist Rick Garvey. However, Rick can't stand the thought that his girlfriend is in love with a boxer. In order to make enough money to live on for himself, Pat, and her father Johnny decides to go for the big fight after all. Pat's dad thinks that Johnny has betrayed the pair of them and suffers a heart attack. Despite his best intentions Johnny is blamed by Pat for the tragedy. Johnny takes part in the fight but loses and in the dressing room afterwards has a barney with Rick. He lands him such a right hook that he permanently hurts his hand. Pat realises he was only thinking of her after all and forgives him, as does Rick.

Behind The Scenes: This was the second of three films made for M-G-M. Marilyn wasn't used at all by the producer and director.

Did You Know?: Marilyn is not listed in the onscreen credits.

What The Critics Say: 'The movies are overdue with a picture like *Right Cross*. It's long past time Hollywood took up the cudgels in defence of the plain old American majority, and it's good to have the shoe on the other foot for a change… outstanding dialogue, a wonderful sense of humour and a talented cast would make it exceptional film fare, with or without the lesson in sociology' *New York Daily News*.

The Verdict: Sentimental fare. 1/5

Hometown Story
(M-G-M, May 1951)

The Crew: Director, Writer & Producer Arthur Pierson. Cinematographer Lucien N Andriot. Editor William F Claxton. Music Louis Forbes. Art Direction Hilyard F Brown.

The Cast: Jeffrey Lynn (Blake Washburn), Donald Crisp (John MacFarland), Marjorie Reynolds (Janice Hunt), Alan Hale, Jr (Slim Haskins), Marilyn Monroe (Iris Martin), Barbara Brown (Mrs Washburn), Melinda Plowman (Katie Washburn), Griff Barnett (Uncle Cliff), Kenny McEvoy (Taxi Driver), Glenn Tryon (Kenlock), 61 minutes.

The Story: Blake Washburn wants to become a politician and run for state office but loses to the son of a wealthy business tycoon. Back home he inherits a newspaper when his uncle retires. He uses the power of the press to wage war against big business.

Behind The Scenes: Another film that Johnny Hyde had to persuade Marilyn would be good public exposure for her.

Did You Know?: The film was financed by General Motors as a paean to big business. Director and writer Arthur Pierson had previously worked with Marilyn on *Dangerous Years*.

What The Critics Say: 'Arthur Pierson wrote and directed, using a competent professional cast... Marilyn Monroe, Barbara Brown and Griff Barnet are up to script demands' *Variety*.

The Verdict: It is obvious where the money is coming from. 1/5

As Young As You Feel
(20th Century-Fox, 2 August 1951)

The Crew: Director Harmon Jones. Writer & Producer Lamar Trotti. Story Paddy Chayefsky. Cinematographer Joseph MacDonald. Editor Robert E Simpson. Music Cyril J Mockridge.

The Cast: Monty Woolley (John Hodges), Thelma Ritter (Della Hodges), David Wayne (Joe Elliott), Jean Peters (Alice Hodges), Constance Bennett (Lucille McKinley), Marilyn Monroe (Harriet), Allyn Joslyn (George Hodges), Albert Dekker (Louis McKinley), Clinton Sundberg (Frank Erickson), Minor Watson (Cleveland), Russ Tamblyn (Willie McKinley), 77 minutes.

The Story: The Acme Printing Services company has a policy of compulsory retirement for employees when they hit 65. John Hodges' daughter's boyfriend suggests he writes a letter to the company President. Fortunately, the company President is a recluse so Hodges impersonates him and visits the company. One of his first tasks is to rescind the ageist policy. A speech he makes causes the company stock to rise which leads to his unmasking. However, the company President, Cleveland, is impressed by Hodges' work and offers him a high-powered job. Hodges is not a high-flyer and all he wants is his old job back.

Behind The Scenes: This was the first film that Marilyn made under the new contract negiotated by Johnny Hyde. It was while making this film that Hyde died of a heart attack. Marilyn was so upset that according to Natasha Lytess she tried to commit suicide.

Did You Know?: The film was also known as *Will You Love Me In December?*

What The Critics Say: 'This unpretentious little picture... is a vastly superior entertainment so far as ingenuity and taste are concerned, and it certainly confronts its audience on a more appropriately adult plane... deft and agile. Albert Dekker is mighty amusing as a fat-headed small business boss, Marilyn Monroe is superb as his secretary' Bosley Crowther, *The New York Times*.

The Verdict: A worthy film. 2/5

Love Nest
(20th Century-Fox, 10 October 1951)

The Crew: Director Joseph M Newman. Writer IAL Diamond. Novel Scott Corbett. Producer Jules Buck. Cinematographer Lloyd Ahern. Editor J Watson Webb, Jr. Music Cyril J Mockridge. Art Direction George Patrick & Lyle R Wheeler.

The Cast: June Haver (Connie Scott), William Lundigan (Jim Scott), Frank Fay (Charley Patterson), Marilyn Monroe (Roberta 'Bobby' Stevens), Jack Paar (Ed Forbes), Leatrice Joy (Eadie Gaynor), Henry Kulky (George Thompson), Marie Blake (Mrs Quigg), Patricia Miller (Florence), Maude Wallace (Mrs Arnold), 84 minutes.

The Story: War veteran Jim Scott buys a home in New York and wants to settle down and write but since he and his wife have a financial stake in the building he is forever at someone's beck and call.

Behind The Scenes: Having signed Marilyn 20th Century-Fox were determined to use her sex appeal even if the film was unworthy of her. This was one such film.

Did You Know?: As a gimmick to raise awareness of the film the studio attached a coupon to publicity posters that could be sent back to Fox for a pin-up of Marilyn.

What The Critics Say: 'There are only a few fresh lines and situations in the script, and they are not enough to add any punch to a rather 'dated' theme, no matter how hard the cast toppers try to keep the laughs going… Marilyn Monroe is tossed in to cause jealousy between the landlords' *Variety*.

The Verdict: Unworthy of Marilyn's talents. 1/5

Let's Make It Legal
(20th Century-Fox, 6 November 1951)

The Crew: Director Richard Sale. Writer IAL Diamond. Story Mortimer Braus. Producer Robert Bassler. Cinematographer Lucien Ballard. Editor Robert Fritch. Music Cyril J Mockridge. Musical Direction Lionel Newman. Art Direction Albert Hogsett & Lyle R Wheeler. Set Decoration Paul S Fox & Thomas Little. Costumes Charles LeMaire & Renie. Orchestration Bernard Mayers & Edward B Powell. Make-Up Ben Nye. Special Photographic Effects Fred Sersen. Sound Harry M Leonard & E Clayton Ward.

The Cast: Claudette Colbert (Miriam Halsworth), Macdonald Carey (Hugh Halsworth), Zachary Scott (Victor Macfarland), Barbara Bates (Barbara Denham), Robert Wagner (Jerry Denham), Marilyn Monroe (Joyce Mannering), Frank Cady (Ferguson), 77 minutes.

The Story: Miriam Halsworth decides to seek a divorce from her husband, Hugh, after 20 years of marriage. He is the PR for a trendy hotel but also an inveterate gambler. Her wealthy ex-boyfriend, Victor Macfarland, comes to stay at the hotel. When he hears of her separation

31

his interest in her is rekindled. Hugh is still in love with Miriam and to make her jealous starts seeing Joyce. She is something of a gold-digger who is after Victor but only for his money. Victor and Miriam decide to get hitched before he has to leave town for a business meeting in Washington. She wonders why they didn't get married twenty years earlier. He confesses that he and Hugh rolled a dice to see who would get Miriam. He lost. Unsurprisingly, she is furious. Hugh has some prize roses which Miriam decides to wreak revenge upon. He decides to look after his roses by digging them up at night but is seen and is arrested. Newspapers report on the incident much to Victor's embarrassment. Miriam tells Victor she doesn't want to marry him after all. He leaves town and Hugh shows Miriam the dice he used to win her affections from Victor twenty years ago. They were loaded so he knew he would win. Miriam falls for him all over again.

Behind The Scenes: It was another film that Marilyn was shoe-horned into – any rôle as long as she is in the film.

Did You Know?: The film was originally entitled *Don't Call Me Mother*. Marilyn had just 14 lines in the 113-page script.

What The Critics Say: 'Marilyn Monroe is voluptuously amusing as a girl on a husband hunt' *Hollywood Reporter*. 'An inconsistent farce that luckily has sufficient saving graces, the predominating benefit being performances and comedy wise co-stars Claudette Colbert and Macdonald Carey. Their presences and a satisfactory amount of bright dialogue counteract a strained farcical situation and the indifferent story... Marilyn Monroe is amusing in a brief rôle as a beautiful shapely blonde who has her eye on Zachary Scott and his millions' Wanda Hale, *New York Daily News*.

The Verdict: Window dressing but very pretty nonetheless. 1/5

3. Sexy: A Streetwalker Of Stunning Proportions

Clash By Night
(RKO, 18 June 1952)

The Crew: Director Fritz Lang. Writer Alfred Hayes. Play Clifford Odets. Producer Harriet Parsons. Cinematographer Nicholas Musuraca. Editor George J Amy. Music Roy Webb. Musical Direction C Bakaleinoff. Art Direction Carroll Clark & Albert S D'Agostino. Set Decoration Jack Mills & Darrell Silvera. Wardrobe Direction Michael Woulfe. Make-Up Mel Berns. Hairstyles Larry Germain. Special Photographic Effects Harold E Wellman. Sound Jean L Speck & Clem Portman.

The Cast: Barbara Stanwyck (Mae Doyle D'Amato), Paul Douglas (Jerry D'Amato), Robert Ryan (Earl Pfeiffer), Marilyn Monroe (Peggy), J Carrol Naish (Uncle Vince), Keith Andes (Joe Doyle), Silvio Minciotti (Papa D'Amato), 105 minutes.

The Story: Mae Doyle comes home after time away, much to the discomfiture of her brother Joe, sibling rivalry and all that. Joe is in love with Peggy who works in the local fish factory. Mae falls in love with Jerry who is the captain of a fishing trawler, they marry and have a kid. Dissatisfied with her home life she begins an affair with Earl, who operates the projector at the local cinema. Jerry finds out what has been going on and confronts his wife and his cuckold before taking to sea with the child. Earl is something of a selfish rotter and tells Mae to forget about her husband and child and stay with him. Seeing Jerry for the rat he is, she rushes after her true love, her husband, and begs for forgiveness.

Behind The Scenes: Journalist Sidney Skolsky was instrumental in getting Marilyn hired for this film, the first in which she was able to show her talent rather than just being hired for window dressing. Marilyn made the film on loan to RKO, the company whose water tower she could see from her orphanage window. During filming she decided to find the orphanage again but couldn't see it because too many buildings were in the way. News of her nude poses broke after filming and gave the movie tremendous publicity. Jerry Wald was telephoned by a man demanding $10,000 or he would reveal to the world that Marilyn had posed for a nude calendar. Wald looked at the calendar and recognised Marilyn at once. He told RKO publicity head Perry Lieber who ignored the blackmailer and went public via friendly United Press International reporter Aline Mosby. Marilyn didn't own a copy of the calendar – she gave away her copy to her press agent Rupert Allan.

Did You Know?: Marilyn suffered from such nerves that she would throw up before each scene and her skin would break out. She was a perfectionist when it came to her work and often insisted on retakes even when director Fritz Lang was happy with the take. The film's producer, Harriet Parsons, was the daughter of the notorious gossip columnist Louella O Parsons. Despite Marilyn's regular tardiness and mistakes in learning her lines, it was Miss Stanwyck who caused the production to be shut down for ten days when she caught pneumonia. *Clash By Night* was the second film Fritz Lang made for Howard Hughes. The bashful billionaire had one of his aides ask Marilyn out and he took her flying. In the air he tried to kiss her but she wasn't impressed by his stubble and the invitation was not repeated. Fritz Lang initially barred Natasha Lytess from his set claiming that only one director was required for each film. Marilyn complained and a compromise was reached.

What The Critics Say: 'Also, on hand, in a minor rôle shapely Marilyn Monroe as a fish-cannery employee who bounces around in a succession of slacks, bathing suits and sweaters' *Time*. 'While Marilyn Monroe is reduced to what is tantamount to a bit rôle, despite her star billing, she does manage to get over her blonde sexiness in one or two scenes, and the film could have used more of her' *Variety*. '*Clash By Night* also gives us a glimpse of Marilyn Monroe and Keith Andes, who play a pair of lovers. Both are quite handsome, but neither can act' *The New Yorker*.

The Verdict: Quite a melodrama despite a somewhat corny plot. 2/5

We're Not Married!
(20th Century-Fox, 12 July 1952)

The Crew: Director Edmund Goulding. Writer Dwight Taylor. Story Jay Dratler & Gina Kaus. Screenplay & Producer Nunnally Johnson. Cinematographer Leo Tover. Editor Louis R Loeffler. Music Cyril J Mockridge. Musical Direction Lionel Newman. Art Direction & Production Design Leland Fuller & Lyle R Wheeler. Set Decoration Claude E Carpenter & Thomas Little. Wardrobe Direction Charles LeMaire. Costumes Eloise Jenson. Special Photographic Effects Ray Kellogg. Orchestration Bernard Mayers. Make-Up Ben Nye. Sound W D Flick. Sound Recordist Roger Heman. Assistant Director Paul Helmick. Hairstyles Helen Turpin.

The Cast: Ginger Rogers (Ramona Gladwyn), Fred Allen (Steve Gladwyn), Victor Moore (Melvin Bush, JP), Marilyn Monroe (Annabel Norris), David Wayne (Jeff Norris), Eve Arden (Katie Woodruff), Paul Douglas (Hector Woodruff), Eddie Bracken (Willie Fisher), Mitzi Gaynor (Patsy Fisher), Louis Calhern (Freddie Melrose), Zsa Zsa Gabor (Eve Melrose), James Gleason (Duffy), Paul Stewart (Attorney Stone), Jane Darwell (Mrs Bush), Lee Marvin (Pinky), 86 minutes.

The Story: Five couples discover they are not actually hitched because the licence of the Justice of the Peace who married them expired shortly before the ceremonies. Gorgeous Annabel Norris, Mrs Mississippi, enters the Mrs America competition but discovers she is ineligible because her marriage is not legally valid.

Behind The Scenes: It was during filming for this film that Marilyn gave the interview to Aline Mosby about her nude calendar.

Did You Know?: David Wayne is the only man to have married Marilyn twice (albeit on film) in *We're Not Married!* and *How To Marry A Millionaire*.

What The Critics Say: 'The Monroe-Wayne scene is pretty light-weight, but shows off the Monroe form to full advantage in a bathing suit, offering certain exploitation for film' *Variety*. 'Nunnally Johnson has a picnic with marriage in *We're Not Married!* at the Roxy, and his good time is shared by all... With David Wayne and Marilyn Monroe (who looks as though she had been carved out of cake by Michelangelo), it becomes a reason for a kitchen-bound husband to demand that his wife drop her busy activities as a beauty contest winner and return to the home' Otis L Guernsey, Jr, *New York Herald Tribune*.

The Verdict: Quite a fun flick. 2/5

Don't Bother To Knock
(20th Century-Fox, 18 July 1952)

The Crew: Director Roy Baker. Writer Daniel Taradash. Novel *Mischief* Charlotte Armstrong. Producer Julian Blaustein. Musical Director Music Lionel Newman. Cinematographer Lucien Ballard, ASC. Art Direction Lyle Wheeler & Richard Irvine. Set Decoration Thomas Little & Paul S Fox. Editor George A Gittens. Wardrobe Direction Charles LeMaire. Costumes Travilla. Orchestration Earle Hagen & Bernard Mayers. Make-Up Ben Nye. Special Photographic Effects Ray Kellogg. Sound Bernard Freericks & Harry M Leonard. Music Lionel Newman, Jerry Goldsmith & Alfred Newman

The Cast: Richard Widmark (Jed Towers), Marilyn Monroe (Nell Forbes), Anne Bancroft (Lyn Lesley), Donna Corcoran (Bunny Jones), Jeanne Cagney (Rochelle), Lurene Tuttle (Ruth Jones), Elisha Cook, Jr (Eddie Forbes), Jim Backus (Peter Jones), Verna Felton (Mrs Ballew), 76 minutes.

The Story: The McKinley Hotel, New York. Lyn Lesley, the bar singer, complains to the barman that her boyfriend, Jed, is late but that may be because she has written him a 'Dear John' letter. However Jed is already in the hotel. Meanwhile, Nell Forbes lands a job as a babysitter thanks to the lift operator, her uncle Eddie. Nell looks after Bunny Jones while her parents attend a do in the ballroom where Mr Jones is to receive an award for his journalistic work. Unbeknown to Lyn, Jed watches her performance before taking a seat at the bar. Upstairs, Nell lacks a certain enthusiasm as a babysitter.

At the end of Lyn's set Jed confronts her, unhappy with her decision to split. She tries to explain herself. Bored, Nell tries Mrs Jones' perfume and jewellery. Jed and Lyn argue before he storms off to his room, 821. He espies Nell dancing across the way. Working out she's in room 809 he calls her but she is naturally suspicious. He tells her his name is Billy. She hangs up on him. Eddie calls on Nell to find her wearing Mrs Jones' clothes. Nell is still in mourning for a dead love and has attempted suicide by slashing her wrists. She promises Eddie she will put her own clothes back on. Instead, when Eddie is gone she attracts the attention of Jed and summons him over. Jed arrives with a bottle of Rye. She spins him a yarn about who she is. He spots Mr Jones' shoes but Nell tells him they belong to her sister's husband. Nell's boyfriend had been killed in 1946 and she transfers her affection for him onto Jed. As they kiss Bunny wakes up and spills the truth. Jed is disappointed by Nell's lying. Nell tells Jed about her sad life until they are interrupted by Bunny's crying. Nell takes the girl to a window and it looks as if she is considering pushing her out. Realising what might be about to happen, Jed grasps Bunny and tells Nell to put her back to bed.

Jed decides to leave to see Lyn but Nell begs him to stay. When she hugs him he spots the scars on her wrists. Eddie turns up and Nell hides Jed in the bathroom. Eddie is angry to find her still in Mrs Jones' clothes and is concerned by Nell's behaviour but she loses it big time. When Eddie realises a man is hiding in the bathroom Nell picks up an umbrella stand and hits him over the head with it. As Jed tends to Eddie, he decides to call a doctor but Eddie won't let him. He asks Jed to leave but as he does he is stopped first by Nell then by the knocking at the door of a nosy, elderly couple. They want to know what has been going on. He creeps into Bunny's darkened room but doesn't notice that she is bound and gagged. Jed escapes via Bunny's room but he is spotted by the elderly woman who calls the house detective.

Lyn is finishing another set as Jed arrives to talk. He tells her about Nell. Bunny crawls off the bed and knocks the phone off the hook. The operator listens in and informs the house detective that something strange is going on. Meantime, Mrs Jones goes up to investigate and screams when she sees what Nell has done to Bunny. They begin to fight as Jed arrives. Eddie tells Jed that Nell has spent three years in an institution in Oregon. Nell makes her escape as the detective arrives and wanders through the lobby until surrounded by hotel workers. Lyn pushes through the crowd and spots the razor blade in Nell's hand. Jed arrives and Nell hands him the blade. The police arrive to take Nell away...

Behind The Scenes: 20th Century-Fox chose this strange tale for Marilyn's first starring rôle. Marilyn was so scared of making a fool of herself on screen that she spent two days and nights working with Natasha Lytess to perfect her acting for the film. *Don't Bother To Knock* was shot with a restricted budget so director Roy Baker only utilised the first take for each scene. Said Richard Widmark: "We had a hell of a time getting her out of her dressing room and onto the set. At first we thought she'd never get anything right and we'd mutter, 'Oh, this is impossible – you can't print this!' But something happened between the lens and the film, and when we looked at the rushes she had the rest of us knocked off the screen!"

Did You Know?: The story on which the movie was based was originally published in *Good Housekeeping* magazine. Marilyn thought she gave one of her best performances in the film. The film was remade in 1991 as *The Sitter*.

What The Critics Say: 'In *Don't Bother To Knock* at the Globe they've thrown Marilyn Monroe into the deep dramatic waters, either sink or swim, and while she doesn't really do either, you might say that she floats. With that figure, what else can she do... but I thought she was surprisingly good, considering her lack of dramatic seasoning and her abundance of showgirl attributes. I could be prejudiced, though' Archer Winsten, *New York Post*. 'It proves conclusively that she is the kind of big star for which exhibitors are always asking' Vincent Conley, *Motion Picture Herald Tribune*. 'It requires a good deal to play a person who is strangely jangled in the head. And, unfortunately, all the equipment that Miss Monroe has to handle the job are a childishly blank expression and a provokingly feeble, hollow voice. With these she makes a game endeavour to pull something out of the rôle, but it looks as though she and her director, Roy Baker, were not quite certain what... All in all, Miss Monroe needs much more practice than she shows in *Don't Bother To Knock*' Bosley Crowther, *The New York Times*.

The Verdict: Marilyn is at once scary but sympathetic as the bewildered soul. As with many of her performances you are left thinking: if only I could have been there, I could have saved her. 4/5

Monkey Business
(20th Century-Fox, 5 September 1952)

The Crew: Director Howard Hawks. Writers Ben Hecht, Charles Lederer & IAL Diamond. Story Harry Segall. Producer Sol C Siegel. Music Leigh Harline. Musical Direction Lionel Newman. Cinematographer Milton R Krasner, ASC. Art Direction Lyle R Wheeler. Set Decoration Thomas Little & Walter M Scott. Editor William B Murphy. Wardrobe Direction Charles LeMaire. Costumes Travilla. Orchestration Earle H Hagen. Make-Up Ben Nye. Special Photographic Effects Ray Kellogg. Sound W D Flick & Roger Heman. Production Designers George Patrick & Lyle R Wheeler. Assistant Director Paul Helmick. Hairstyles Helen Turpin.

The Cast: Cary Grant (Barnaby Fulton), Ginger Rogers (Edwina Fulton), Charles Coburn (Mr Oliver Oxley), Marilyn Monroe (Lois Laurel), Hugh Marlowe (Hank Entwhistle), Henri Letondal (Siegfried Kitzel), Robert Cornthwaite (Dr Zoldeck), Larry Keating (GJ Culverly), Douglas Spencer (Dr Brunner), Esther Dale (Mrs Rhinelander), Harry Carey, Jr (Journalist), 97 minutes.

The Story: Dr Barnaby Fulton is a forgetful man with poor eyesight necessitating extra thick spectacles. Naturally, he is also the most brilliant scientist of his generation working to develop a youth serum. Edwina is his ever-loving, ever-patient wife who doesn't mind his absent-mindedness. Deciding not to go to a yacht club party, their friend and lawyer Hank Entwhistle (who is also secretly in love with Edwina) arrives at 1605 Gilcrest to find out why. Unwittingly, Barnaby thinks he has discovered the answer to the puzzle that has been bothering him. At work he is summoned to see the boss Mr Oxley and wonders why his secretary, the gorgeous Miss Laurel, is already at her desk. "Mr Oxley has been complaining about my punctuation so I'm careful to get here before nine," she replies malapropistically. She is wearing his experimental, acetate, non-ladder stockings and lifts her skirt to show him her shapely stocking-clad pins. Later in Oxley's office the boss hands Miss Laurel a draft letter and asks her to get someone to type it. "Oh Mr Oxley, can't I try again?" she plaintively asks but he tells her no, get someone to do it for her.

Then news comes from the laboratory that Rudolph, an 84-year-old chimp, has escaped from his cage after taking some of Barnaby's formula. Sadly, it turns out to be a case of mistaken identity and the energetic simian is only Esther, 6-months old. Barnaby goes back to work but when he leaves the lab Esther again breaks out of her cage and mixes up a batch of something or other, drinks some and then puts the rest of the mixture into the temporarily empty water fountain. Barnaby returns to the lab, tests some of his potion and then has a drink from the water fountain. He begins to feel dizzy before his pulse increases to 150. He removes his thick glasses and finds he can see properly for the first time in years. Feeling youthful once again, he climbs out of the window and goes off for a new haircut, suit and a sports car. Oxley sends Miss Laurel to track down the errant scientist and she comes across him buying a new sports car. He takes her for a spin in the car, crashes it and while it is in for repair (to be collected later that day – some mechanic!!) swimming and roller skating. Back in the car she kisses him and tells him she fancies him. But then the potion wears off and, without his glasses, Barnaby goes nearly blind. He tells Edwina of his day and she decides to test his formula again, washed down with the requisite glass of water. Under the influence, she puts a goldfish down Oxley's trousers, threatens to deck Miss Laurel for flirting with Barnaby and then insists Barnaby take her to Room 304 at the Pickwick Hotel where they spent their honeymoon. The immaturity of youth kicks in and they fight during which she steps on Barnaby's glasses and locks him out of their room. Somehow he ends up in a laundry chute.

In the morning Edwina is back to her old self and drives them home where they are met by the press. In her youthful state she has rung Hank to tell him to file for divorce and cried to her mother. Both are also waiting for her. Barnaby decides he has had enough and at the lab rips up the formula. He and Edwina drink lots of coffee made with the contaminated water. Meanwhile, Oxley calls a board meeting to arrange to buy the rights to the formula from Barnaby. When the Fultons are summoned to the meeting they arrive hand-in-hand with a chimp, having reverted to the behavioural patterns of 10-year-olds. They run away and indulge in childish games like covering themselves in paint. Edwina again rings Hank while Barnaby goes off to play Red Indians with a group of children. Their next-door neighbour is asked to look after a small boy and places him for some reason in the Fultons' backyard. The boy stands up and his nappy falls off and he wanders into the Fultons' bedroom where he climbs onto the bed next to Edwina. She wakes and thinks the formula has had a dramatic effect on Barnaby and rushes him to the lab. Hank arrives, is tied to a tree by the kids and scalped by Barnaby whom the kids nickname Red Eagle. At the lab GJ Culverly doesn't believe the baby is Barnaby but they think if they let him sleep he will revert to his old self. While they are waiting they down some whisky and, guess what?, contaminated water. Barnaby climbs into his lab via the window and lays down on his couch next to 'baby Barnaby.' Outside the potion is beginning to take effect…

Behind The Scenes: Fox boss Darryl F Zanuck had described Monroe as "empty-headed" so the screenwriters decided to play a subtle joke on their boss by having Marilyn play the only sane character in the film. Screenwriter Ben Hecht persuaded Marilyn to write her memoirs, serialised in the *Empire News* but not published in book form until 12 years after her death. However, Hecht knew much of what she told him was fictitious. In February 1952 she was introduced to baseball legend Joe DiMaggio. Their first date was at the Villa Nova restaurant at 9015 Sunset Boulevard. On 1 March 1952, during filming, Marilyn was diagnosed with appendicitis but rather than delay production she opted to put surgery on hold. That same day Fox's PR department became aware of Marilyn's nude calendar. Marilyn chose to brave out the storm giving one journalist, Aline Mosby of the Los *Angeles Herald-Examiner*, an exclusive on the story of how she was broke and hungry when she posed for Tom Kelley. The strategy worked and Marilyn weathered a storm that could have killed her career stone dead.

Did You Know?: The film was also known as *Be Your Age* and *Darling I Am Growing Younger*. The première was held in Atlantic City, New Jersey (home of the Miss America beauty pageant), and as a publicity stunt Marilyn was asked to become the first ever Grand Marshal in September 1952.

What The Critics Say: 'Marilyn Monroe, described by Grant as "half-child" and counter-described by Rogers with "not the visible half," poses and walks in a manner that must be called suggestive. What she suggests is something that this picture seems to have on its mind much of the time with or without the rejuvenation' Paul V Beckley, *New York Herald Tribune*. 'Marilyn Monroe can look and act dumber than any of the screen's current blondes' Kate Cameron, *New York Daily News*.

The Verdict: *Monkey Business* does age well. Parts of it are overdone but for the most part it is still an amusing film and thus gets 3 out of 5.

O Henry's Full House
(20th Century-Fox, 16 October 1952)

The Crew: Director Henry Koster. Writer Lamarr Trotti. Producer André Hakim. Cinematographer Lloyd Ahern. Editor Nick DeMaggio. Music Alfred Newman.

The Cast: John Steinbeck (Narrator), Charles Laughton (Soapy), Marilyn Monroe (Streetwalker), David Wayne (Horace), Richard Karlan (Head waiter), Erno Verebes (Waiter), 117 minutes.

The Story: This film is an anthology of stories by famed American writer O Henry (born as William Sydney Porter, he wrote many of his stories in prison while serving time for embezzlement of funds from the bank where he worked), the film was released with the tagline: 'A dozen top stars - five famed directors bring you the best stories of O Henry!' In Marilyn's segment *The Cop And The Anthem*, the first of the five, she plays a hooker but is only on screen for about a minute. Laughton is a tramp who tries to get himself arrested so he can have a warm bed and food. He smashes a window, eats a meal he can't pay for in a restaurant and finally accosts a woman hoping she will scream only to find out she is on the game. Charmed by her, he gives her his umbrella and she bursts into tears.

Behind The Scenes: On 28 April Marilyn underwent the appendectomy, performed by Dr Marcus Rabwin. Whilst prepping her for surgery, he was surprised to discover a note taped to her stomach. It read: 'Dear Dr Rabwin, Cut *as little* as possible. I know it seems vain but that doesn't really enter into it. The fact that I'm a *woman* is important and means much to me. Save please (I can't ask you enough) what you can – I'm in your hands. You have children and you must know *what* it means – *please Dr Rabwin* – I know somehow you *will*! *Thank you* – *thank you* – *thank you*. For God's sake Dear Doctor No *ovaries* removed – please again do whatever you can to prevent large scars. Thanking you with all my *heart*. *Marilyn Monroe*.'

Did You Know?: Joe DiMaggio was furious with Fox for casting Marilyn as a prostitute.

What The Critics Say: 'Marilyn Monroe, again as sleek as she was in *The Asphalt Jungle*, is a streetwalker of stunning proportions' Archer Winsten, *New York Post*.

The Verdict: A touching film. 3/5

4. Fun: A Giggle In Her Talk

Niagara
(20th Century-Fox, 21 January 1953)

The Crew: Director Henry Hathaway. Writers Charles Brackett, Walter Reisch & Richard Breen. Producer Charles Brackett. Cinematographer Joe MacDonald, ASC. Editor Barbara McLean, ACE. Music Sol Kaplan. Musical Direction Lionel Newman. Art Direction Maurice Ransford & Lyle Wheeler. Set Decorations Stuart Reiss. Wardrobe Direction Charles LeMaire. Costumes Dorothy Jeakins. Orchestration Edward Powell. Make-Up Artist Ben Nye. Special Photographic Effects Ray Kellogg. Sound W D Flick & Roger Heman. Assistant Director Gerd Oswald.

The Cast: Marilyn Monroe (Rose Loomis), Joseph Cotten (George Loomis), Jean Peters (Polly Cutler), Casey Adams (Ray Cutler), Denis O'Dea (Inspector Starkey), Richard Allan (Ted Patrick), Don Wilson (J C Kettering), Lurene Tuttle (Mrs Kettering), Harry Carey, Jr (Taxi driver), 89 minutes.

The Story: Ray Cutler works for a shredded wheat manufacturer in Toledo, Ohio, and wins a cash prize for coming up with a snappy slogan in a competition. He uses the money to take Polly, his wife of three years, on a belated honeymoon to Niagara Falls. Arriving at the Rainbow Cabins they find their cabin, B, has not been vacated by the previous incumbents, Rose and George Loomis, so the Cutlers are billeted in cabin K.

George is in love with Rose but she finds solace elsewhere and, to add to his problems, he has only recently been released from an army mental institution. Rose tells George she is going shopping. During a visit to the Scenic Tunnel under the Falls, Polly spots Rose in a fond embrace with her lover, Ted Patrick. Back at the cabins, Rose takes a shower and George asks her where the cigarettes are. Searching her coat for them, he discovers the ticket stub for the Scenic Tunnel. He keeps his own counsel. Outside a party is being held and Rose joins them bringing a copy of a record, *Kiss*, with her. George watches from behind the cabin's blind. Rose joins the Cutlers and sings along to the record until her husband comes out and, grabbing the record, smashes it cutting his hand in the process. Polly gets the first-aid kit and goes to him. George tells her of his misfortunes before smashing the model car he has been making.

That night Rose plots with Ted to murder George. The next morning Rose and George argue before Rose storms out - supposedly to buy bus tickets for the journey home to Chicago, but in reality to meet Ted. When George arrives at the Union Bus Terminal there is no sign of Rose. He hurries to Niagara Falls where Rose is meeting her lover in the gift shop. George buys a ticket for the Scenic Tunnel and is followed by Ted.

Back at the Rainbow Cabins, Rose asks the Cutlers if they have seen her husband. They report him missing to the police and Detective Starkey meets them at the Falls. The cop finds a solitary pair of shoes at the changing room and Rose identifies them as belonging to George. The Cutlers offer Rose a lift back to the cabins but as she gets in the car the bells begin to play *Kiss* which is the signal from Ted to let Rose know he has been successful. The authorities find a corpse but when Rose goes to identify it, she faints and is hospitalised.

The head of Ray's shredded wheat company, JC Kettering, and his wife arrive at the Rainbow Cabins to meet the Cutlers. Ray is away and eventually Mrs Kettering persuades her overeager husband that Polly might want some peace. The Cutlers have been moved into cabin B and Polly lays down on one of the beds - in the puritanical 1950s the rooms had two single beds, even for married couples - and tries to get some sleep. George comes back to the cabin thinking Rose is in the bed, grabs a knife from the kitchen. Half asleep, she screams and frightens him away. Ray arrives and comforts his wife. Polly tells him Loomis is still alive. Fed up, Ray announces they are leaving until Polly mentions the visit by the Ketterings. While Ray has a shave, Polly calls Inspector Starkey but her call is overheard by Loomis.

On a visit by the Cutlers and Ketterings to the Falls, JC decides he knows more than the guide and takes Ray off on a private excursion. Mrs Kettering disappears for a crafty cigarette leaving Polly alone. Alone that is except for Loomis who chases after her, nearly causing her to fall into the foaming water. He tells her he killed Ted in an act of self-defence and asks her to keep his secret but she tells him to go to the police. Inspector Starkey has let himself into the Cutlers' cabin and tells them Rose has flitted from the hospital. Then Polly tells him Loomis is still alive.

Rose, meanwhile, has made her way to the bus station and after getting a refund ($12.50) on a ticket to Chicago heads for the terminal. Once there she hears a married couple moaning about delays caused by police checks. A taxi driver is no more helpful blaming "smugglers or something." Deciding to get back to America on foot, Rose bumps into George and runs away. He follows her at a distance and catches up with her in the bell tower where he strangles her. Downstairs, he discovers he has been locked in and goes back upstairs to spend the night

43

with his wife's corpse. He tells her he loves her. Making his escape in the morning, he unsuccessfully tries to hire a boat. The Cutlers and Ketterings have been on a fishing trip and more to get fresh supplies. While they are ashore, George steals onto their boat but Polly comes back alone. They struggle and she is knocked unconscious. He leaves the berth with Polly aboard. Chased by the US River Patrol, the boat runs out of petrol but not before it is captured by the main current heading for the Falls. George attempts to scuttle the boat as the Air Sea Rescue helicopter is launched. Heading for some rocks, he throws Polly onto them to be rescued by the helicopter before facing his own fate as the boat crashes over Niagara Falls to his certain death.

Behind The Scenes: While filming *Niagara* Marilyn was asked to pose for photographs by a 25-year-old fan from Marion, Ohio. His name was Robert F Slatzer. He disappeared publicly from Marilyn's story until 1972 when he approached journalist Will Fowler (the son of the writer Gene Fowler, once the tenth highest-paid person in the USA) with a story that Marilyn's death was the result of a political conspiracy. Slatzer wanted Fowler's help into turning his work into a book. Fowler was unimpressed by Slatzer: "I said to him: 'Too bad you weren't married to Monroe. That would really make a good book.' After I had gotten into the first draft, Slatzer mentioned that he had been married to Marilyn, but 'only for a weekend.'" Fowler became suspicious and asked for his name to be removed from the book. The book was published under the title *The Life & Curious Death Of Marilyn Monroe* in 1974. It was rewritten by George Carpozi, Jr, a journalist who had extensively interviewed Marilyn. Fowler adds: "Until recently I considered Slatzer to be a harmless faker... Take this from the one who removed his name from the book: Robert Slatzer was never married to Marilyn Monroe. He met the star only once. That was in Niagara Falls, New York, where he had his only pictures taken with her while she was making the movie, *Niagara*...Slatzer never met Marilyn before or since that time." Slatzer claims that he and Marilyn were married in Tijuana on 4 October 1952, having travelled down to Mexico the day before. During research for his biography of Marilyn, best-selling author Donald Spoto discovered a cheque written by Marilyn for $313.13 payable to Jax, a shop on Wilshire Boulevard. Marilyn had bought various garments and accessories. Underneath her signature she listed her current address: 2393 Castilian Drive, Outpost Estates, Hollywood Hills. If Slatzer is to be believed, Marilyn drove down to Mexico with him on Friday evening and then while he and she were being married, Marilyn was also able to be in Los Angeles with Natasha Lytess doing what so many women like to do on a Saturday afternoon — buying clothes.

Did You Know?: The rôle of Polly Cutler was originally intended for Anne Baxter but she withdrew from the film and Jean Peters was cast in her stead. When the recasting occurred, the film was altered to feature Marilyn more prominently. The film contains what was then the longest walk (Marilyn's) in celluloid history — 116 feet. The camera is trained on Marilyn's backside for the entire stroll. Director Henry Hathaway was not looking forward to the assignment. He had heard Marilyn could be 'difficult.' He was delighted to discover that Marilyn was a joy to work with. "Joe [DiMaggio] was there to keep her happy," he said. The walls of the cathedral of pop culture in Ken Russell's film *Tommy* (1975) are covered in huge stills of Marilyn including some from *Niagara*. Sequences in Jonathan Demme's Hitchcockian thriller *Last Embrace* (1979) owe more than a little to *Niagara*.

What The Critics Say: 'Miss Monroe plays the kind of wife whose dress, in the words of the script, 'is cut so low you can see her knees.' The dress is red: the actress has very nice knees, and under Hathaway's direction she gives the kind of serpentine performance that makes the audience hate her while admiring her, which is proper for the story' Otis L Guernsey, Jr, *New York Herald Tribune*. 'Miss Monroe is vulgar and faintly repulsive' *The Monthly Film Bulletin*. 'What lifts the film above the commonplace is its star, Marilyn Monroe' *Time*.

The Verdict: *Niagara* was the film that made Marilyn a star. It is a vivid portrayal of jealousy, infidelity and certainly went against the social mores of the time. 4/5

Gentlemen Prefer Blondes
(20th Century-Fox, 15 July 1953)

The Crew: Director Howard Hawks. Writer Charles Lederer. Play Joseph Fields & Anita Loos. Novel Anita Loos. Producer Sol C Siegel. Cinematographer Harry J Wild. Editor Hugh S Fowler. Art Direction Lyle R Wheeler & Joseph C Wright. Set Decoration Claude E Carpenter. Wardrobe Direction Charles LeMaire. Costumes Travilla. Music Lionel Newman, Leo Robin & Jule Styne. Orchestration Bernard Mayers & Herbert W Spencer. Make-Up Ben Nye. Choreographer Jack Cole. Vocal Director Eliot Daniel. Colour Consultant Leonard Doss. Assistant Director Paul Helmick. Sound Roger Heman & E Clayton Ward.

The Cast: Jane Russell (Dorothy Shaw), Marilyn Monroe (Lorelei Lee), Charles Coburn (Sir Francis Beekman), Elliott Reid (Detective Malone), Tommy Noonan (Gus Esmond), George Winslow (Henry Spofford III), Marcel Dalio (Magistrate),

Taylor Holmes (Esmond, Sr), Norma Varden (Lady Beekman), Howard Wendell (Watson), Harry Carey, Jr (Winslow), George Chakiris (Dancer), 91 minutes.

The Story: Gus Esmond is a rich young swain who is engaged to blonde showgirl Lorelei Lee. His father thinks she is a no good gold-digger and employs Malone, a private detective, to follow her. Lorelei and her brunette friend, Dorothy Shaw, travel to Paris for the wedding via a boat and Malone is on their tails. Aboard Dorothy falls for Malone. He manages to take a picture of Lorelei being hugged by ageing diamond merchant Sir Francis Beekman. However, the 'hug' is innocent. He is actually showing her how a python kills a goat!! The girls determine to get the incriminating picture back and do so by slipping Malone a Micky Finn. Sir Francis is also relieved that he won't be involved in a scandal and gives Lorelei a diamond tiara belonging to his wife as a sign of his gratitude. In Paris Gus' father believes his suspicions have proved correct and the two girls find themselves broke. To make some money they land jobs in a nightclub. Meantime, Lady Beekman realises her tiara is missing and alerts the authorities who regard Lorelei as the prime suspect. Dorothy dons a blonde wig and takes Lorelei's place in court so her chum can go and see Gus to persuade him that she really does love him for himself and not for his riches. Malone discovers that Sir Francis was the real thief and presents this evidence to the court. Dorothy falls for him once more and Gus and (his doubting) father finally believe Lorelei. Cue two weddings…

Behind The Scenes: Marilyn learned she had won the coveted rôle of Lorelei Lee on her 26th birthday, 1 June 1952. Originally the part was earmarked for Betty Grable but Darryl Zanuck gave the casting vote to Marilyn after hearing her sing *Do It Again*. Marilyn was also favoured because her contract with 20th Century-Fox meant that she came much cheaper than Grable. Although they were rivals in the film, off-screen Marilyn and Jane Russell were very friendly. Musical director Lionel Newman opined: "She was damned sure of what she wanted. The men in the orchestra adored her. She was always congenial, courteous, not temperamental, and never forgot to thank everyone who worked with her."

Did You Know?: Anita Loos' novel was filmed for the first time in 1928 starring Ruth Taylor and Alice White. It cost 20th Century-Fox $500,000 to obtain the rights to the book. The outfit for *Diamonds Are A Girl's Best Friend* was originally much more revealing than the strapless pink one Marilyn eventually donned for the number. A fear of the censor's scissors forced the change. Marilyn insisted on eleven takes for *Bye Bye Baby* even though director Howard Hawks was happy with the first one. Marilyn added a line to the script herself. Her wealthy boyfriend's father says: "I thought you were dumb." Lorelei replies: "I can be smart when it's important, but most men don't like it." Marilyn won *Photoplay* magazine's Best Actress of 1953 for her part as Lorelei.

What The Critics Say: 'And there is Marilyn Monroe! Zounds, boys, what a personality this one is! Send up a happy flare. At last, she is beautifully gowned, beautifully coiffed, and a wonderful crazy humour flashes from those sleepy eyes of hers' Ruth Waterbury, *The Los Angeles Examiner*. 'Putting these two buxom pin-up girls in the same movie is merely giving 2-1 odds on a sure thing, and the pay-off is big in a rousing musical... Singing, dancing or just staring at diamonds, these girls are irresistible and their musical is as lively as a sting of firecrackers on the Fourth of July... As usual, Miss Monroe looks like she would glow in the dark, and her version of the baby-faced blonde whose eyes open for diamonds and close for kisses is always amusing as well as alluring' Otis Guernsey, Jr, *The New York Herald Tribune*. 'It is an empty and graceless remake of a fair to middling musical that only comes alive when Marilyn Monroe and Jane Russell stop talking and start wriggling' Hollis Albert, *Saturday Review*. 'As Lorelei Lee, Marilyn looks as delectable as a ripe peach. She also surprised with a remarkably stylish voice piping *Diamonds Are A Girl's Best Friend* in a lavish production number' Margaret Hartford, *The Los Angeles Citizen News*.

The Verdict: This film is a fun frolic, with Marilyn showing her musical talents. 3/5

How To Marry A Millionaire
(20th Century-Fox, 10 November 1953)

The Crew: Director Jean Negulesco. Writer Nunnally Johnson. Plays Zoe Akins & Dale Eunson & Katherine Albert. Title Doris Lilly. Producer Nunnally Johnson. Musical Direction Alfred Newman. Incidental Music Cyril Mockridge. Cinematographer Joe MacDonald, ASC. Art Direction Lyle Wheeler & Leland Fuller. Set Decoration Walter M Scott & Stuart Reiss. Special Photographic Effects Ray Kellogg. Editor Louis Loeffler. Wardrobe Direction Charles LeMaire. Costumes Travilla. Orchestration Edward B Powell. Make-Up Ben Nye. Sound Alfred Bruzlin & Roger Heman. Assistant Director FE 'Johnny' Johnston. Technicolor Colour Consultant Leonard Doss. *Street Scene* Composer/Conductor Alfred Newman.

The Cast: Betty Grable (Loco Dempsey), Marilyn Monroe (Pola Debevoise), Lauren Bacall (Schatze Page), David Wayne (Freddie Denmark), Rory Calhoun

(Eben), Cameron Mitchell (Tom Brookman), Alexander D'Arcy (J Stewart Merrill),
Fred Clark (Waldo Brewster), William Powell (JD Hanley), 95 minutes.

The Story: New York: three gold-digging models rent an expensive
apartment at Sutton Place South and East 55th Street in a bid to land
rich husbands. Their rent is $1,000 a month. Schatze Page is cynical
about men mainly due to bad experiences with her recent ex-husband.
Pola Debevoise is the blonde bombshell who never wears her spectacles because she believes that men don't make passes at girls who wear
glasses. Consequently, she bumps into things as she is blind as a bat
without them. Loco Dempsey has a way of getting men to buy things
for her. Her most recent 'victim' is Tom Brookman whom she meets at
the cold cuts counter of the local deli. The girls finance the apartment
by selling all the furniture.

Tom keeps calling to ask Schatze out but, thinking he is poor, she
turns him down. He is really a multi-millionaire. Loco meets 56-year-
old Dallas cattle baron JD Handley at the mink counter of a major store
and he invites the girls to an oil barons party. Schatze persuades JD to
leave the Oil Institute and take her to a posh restaurant. Loco hooks up
with Waldo Brewster and while eating at the same restaurant as
Schatze he invites her to his lodge in Maine. Pola is also in the same
eatery with J Stewart Merrill but she is bored by him until he mentions
he is worth $200-$300 million. Meanwhile, Tom goes to the fashion
house Antoine's and tells him to arrange a show but insists he hire
Schatze. Also working are Loco and Pola. Brewster takes Loco to the
snow-capped mountains of Maine and his lodge. She thinks his lodge
is a convention and only when they arrive does she realise he means his
snow lodge. (The film contains a number of in-jokes. Brewster
switches on the wireless and a big band is heard. Loco identifies them
wrongly as Harry James. Betty Grable was, of course, married to Harry
James.) At the lodge she comes down with a fever of 102, the measles
and has to stay for a week.

Back in New York Freddie Denmark, the flat's owner, who had to
flee because he hadn't paid income tax sneaks back into the apartment
and is amazed to find all his furniture gone. While he is trying to open
his safe Schatze comes back early with JD. Denmark hides on the bal-
cony in the pouring rain and finds himself locked out. Inside JD tells
Schatze he is going back to Dallas because he's too old for her. Schatze
insists she likes older men: "Look at Roosevelt! Look at Churchill!
Look at that old fellow, what's his name, in *The African Queen*." (Lau-

48

ren Bacall was married to the much older Humphrey Bogart, star of *The African Queen*.) As Denmark finally makes his escape, Pola arrives. She tells Schatze that she and Stewart are to be married. In Maine, Loco goes skiing and more with Eben who chauffeured her and Brewster while Brewster comes down with the measles. She believes Eben is rich. Back in New York Denmark again tries to reach his safe and is amazed to find the place is now furnished thanks to JD's generosity. The phone rings as he gets the documents from the safe. Pola rushes in to answer the phone but *sans* specs thinks Denmark is a friend of Schatze. Pola flies down to Atlantic City to meet Stewart's mum and finds Denmark sitting next to her on the plane. They recognise each other and sympathise with the other's poor vision. Denmark persuades Pola to put her glasses on. He tells her she looks much better with the specs on. He reveals how he was cheated by his accountant and is going to Kansas City to have it out with him. Then Pola realises that she is on the wrong flight.

Eben takes Loco to his shack and it is there she realises he isn't rich after all and is, in fact, a park ranger. She's in love with him but can't hide her disappointment. Brewster decides to drive back to New York so he won't be seen by anyone who knows him. As they cross the George Washington Bridge, they are stopped by motorcycle police. They are apparently the 50 millionth couple to drive across the bridge and the press are there to record the happy moment. Back in the apartment Schatze again sells the piano. Tom calls yet again and finally Schatze agrees to have dinner with him. They go to a hamburger emporium and, the next day, visit the Statue of Liberty. All the time Schatze is telling him that she likes him but can't be with him because he doesn't have any money. Despite this she falls for him but in the meantime hocks the rest of her furniture. JD returns as the removal men are leaving and she immediately calls the doorman to get him to return the furnishings. She agrees to marry JD. Loco turns up half an hour before the ceremony to tell Schatze she is married. Then Pola arrives to tell Schatze she is also married, to Denmark. The ceremony is about to begin when Schatze feigns a weak ankle. She tells JD she's in love with Tom but believes he is a petrol pump attendant. JD knows who Tom really is and tells him that Schatze is in love with him. The three models and their three husbands go to another hamburger joint where they discuss money. Eben says he is worth $14 while Denmark still has his woes with the bent accountant. They laugh when Tom says he is

49

worth $200 million until he pays the bill with a $1,000 note and tells the chef to keep the change...

Behind The Scenes: The gossips believed that Monroe and Grable would hate each other as the reigning queen of the Fox lot (Grable) was being replaced by the young pretender (Monroe) but it never happened. The two women got on extremely well even to the extent of painting Marilyn's toenails when the press arrived to see her.

Did You Know?: *How To Marry A Millionaire* was the first film ever made in wide-screen CinemaScope although it was actually released after the second, *The Robe*. Marilyn wanted to play the rôle of Loco because she didn't want to be seen on-screen in glasses. For the première on 4 November 1953, she had to be sewn into her dress and got drunk at the party beforehand through nerves. The film cost $2.5 million to make but the outlay was recouped five times over within months of opening.

What The Critics Say: 'Betty Grable, Lauren Bacall and Marilyn Monroe give off the quips and cracks, generously supplied by Nunnally Johnson, with a naturalness that adds to their strikingly humorous effect, making the film the funniest comedy of the year' *New York Daily News*. 'The big question 'How does Marilyn Monroe look stretched across a big screen?' is easily answered. If you insisted on sitting in the front row, you would probably feel you were being smothered in Baked Alaska. From any normal vantage point, though, her magnificent proportions are as appealing as ever, and her stint as a deadpan comedienne is as nifty as her looks. Playing a near-sighted charmer who won't wear her glasses when men are around, she bumps into the furniture and reads books upside down with a limpid guile that nearly melts the screen... *How To Marry A Millionaire* is measured, not in square feet, but in the size of the Johnson-Negulesco comic invention and the shape of Marilyn Monroe – and that is about as sizeable and shapely as you can get' Otis L Guernsey, Jr, *New York Herald Tribune*.

The Verdict: As always Marilyn is a delight. Pola is gorgeously sexy and adorable. Betty Grable in the twilight of her glamour days is likeable. Personally, I find Lauren Bacall's character irritating so, for this reason and this reason alone, I award the film 2/5.

River Of No Return
(20th Century-Fox, 30 April 1954)

The Crew: Director Otto Preminger. Writer Frank Fenton. Story Louis Lantz. Producer Stanley Rubin. Cinematographer Joseph LaShelle. Editor Louis R Loeffler. Music Cyril J Mockridge & Lionel Newman. Musical Direction Lionel Newman. Orchestration Edward B Powell. Wardrobe Direction Charles LeMaire. Costumes Charles LeMaire & Travilla. Make-Up Ben Nye. Set Decoration Chester L Bayhi & Walter M Scott. Choreographer Jack Cole. Vocal Direction Ken Darby. Sound Bernard Freericks & Roger Heman. Art Direction Addison Hehr & Lyle R Wheeler. Assistant Director Paul Helmick. Special Photographic Effects Ray Kellogg.

The Cast: Robert Mitchum (Matt Calder), Marilyn Monroe (Kay Weston), Rory Calhoun (Harry Weston), Tommy Rettig (Mark Calder), Murvyn Vye (Colby), Douglas Spencer (Benson), 91 minutes.

The Story: Kay Weston is a singer in a saloon in a frontier town. 10-year-old Mark Calder has a crush on her. His father, Matt, was imprisoned after shooting a man in the back, to save a friend. He purchases a farm to live on with Mark. One day he rescues Kay and her boyfriend, Harry Weston, from a raft. Showing his gratitude Weston steals Calder's horse and sets off for town to file a gold claim. Then Calder's farm is subjected to attack by angry Red Indians. The only way out is via raft. They battle Red Indians, footpads and the elements. Calder is unhappy with Kay's presence primarily because it was her fault that his son's life is now in danger. Eventually, Kay falls in love with Matt but lets slip to Mark the real reason for his dad's jailing. Catching up with Harry Weston, Calder seeks his revenge…

Behind The Scenes: Marilyn didn't get on with director Otto Preminger. He forbade Natasha Lytess' presence on the set until he was ordered to relent by the brass at Fox. Marilyn was liked by the crew for her professionalism. Special effects wizard Paul Wurtzel reported: "We put her through a lot on that film, and there was never one complaint. She knew what the picture required, and once we got her on her marks she was a pro. The whole crew adored her." On 20 August 1953 Marilyn and Robert Mitchum were filming a scene on a raft when Marilyn fell off into the River Athabasca. She hurt her ankle and hobbled around on crutches for a while, delaying filming. When Joe DiMaggio learned of her injury he flew to Canada to comfort her.

Did You Know?: *River Of No Return* was Marilyn's 22nd film in six years. The original concept for producer Stanley Rubin was to make an American version of the Italian movie *The Bicycle Thief* with the lead's gun and horse stolen instead of the bike. The film was shot in Canada and Marilyn stayed at the Banff Springs Hotel on Spray Avenue, Banff.

What The Critics Say: 'There's no doubt Miss Monroe means every bit of business that she's required to do in the adventure yarn, but the heavily dramatic elements of the film are just a little too much for her at this point in her acting career' Lynn Bowers, *Los Angeles Examiner*. 'It's a toss-up whether the scenery or the adornment of Marilyn Monroe is the feature of greater attraction' Bosley Crowther, *New York Times*.

The Verdict: Marilyn looks fab and so does the scenery. 3/5

There's No Business Like Show Business
(20th Century-Fox, 16 December 1954)

The Crew: Director Walter Lang. Writers Henry Ephron & Phoebe Ephron. Story Lamar Trotti. Producer Sol C Siegel. Lyrics & Music Irving Berlin. Dances & Musical Numbers Stager Robert Alton. Associate Jack Cole. Music Supervisors & Conductors Alfred Newman & Lionel Newman. Vocal Supervisor Ken Darby. Orchestration Bernard Mazell, Herbert Spencer, Edward B Powell & Earle Hagen. Vocal Arrangements Ken Darby & Hal Schaefer. Cinematographer Leon Shamroy, ASC. Art Direction Lyle Wheeler & John DeCuir. Set Decoration Walter M Scott & Stuart Reiss. Special Photographic Effects Ray Kellogg. Editor Robert Simpson, ACE. Wardrobe Charles LeMaire. Costumes Miles White & Travilla. Make-up Ben Nye. Hairstyles Helen Turpin. Sound E Clayton Wood & Murray Spivak. Assistant Director Ad Schaumer. Colour Consultant Leonard Doss.

The Cast: Ethel Merman (Molly Donahue), Donald O'Connor (Tim Donahue), Marilyn Monroe (Vicky Hoffman/Parker), Dan Dailey (Terence Donahue), Johnnie Ray (Father Steve Donahue), Mitzi Gaynor (Katy Donahue), Richard Eastham (Lew Harris), Hugh O'Brian (Charles Biggs), Frank McHugh (Eddie Duggan), Rhys Williams (Father Dineen), George Chakiris (Dancer), 117 minutes.

The Story: Vaudeville, 1919, and topping the bill are the Donahues – husband and wife Molly and Terry, a song and dance act. At the end of the show they introduce the latest member of the family. Four years later, there are two more additions to the family but Molly is unhappy about bringing up children on the road and enrols them in St Michael's, a Catholic school in Boston. They begin a new act but the younger Donahues are unhappy and are caught sneaking out of school. Headmaster Father Dineen calls the Donahues in to see him and explains the children miss their parents and miss their old life. The kids go home to their new house in Jersey but the Great Depression soon hits and the family struggles to make ends meet.

In 1937 they reform as The Five Donahues. Tim meets beautiful blonde Vicky Hoffman who is working in the cloakroom of a nightclub 'between engagements' – trouble is, it has been six months since her last engagement. Her agent has persuaded showbiz big shot Lew Harris to visit the club and Vicky has persuaded the management and the band to let her sing. Harris is impressed. On a pretext to get into her dressing room Tim pretends to be Kirby of *Variety* and asks for an interview. Lew Harris recognises Tim and Vicky throws him out. Steve has a bombshell for his parents: he wants to be a priest.

The Four Donahues move to Florida for a gig where they are supported by Vicky now called Vicky Parker. It turns out that *Heat Wave* is due to be performed by both supporting and main acts. Tim, very generously, gives the number to Vicky, much to his mother's annoyance. He falls for her heavily. Lew Harris wants to sign the younger Donahues for his big Broadway show *Manhattan Parade* which is to star Vicky. At Steve's ordination Charles Biggs proposes to Katy who accepts. Tim thinks Vicky is having an affair with Lew Harris and in a drunken stupor he is involved in a car accident and hospitalised. Molly stands in for her son but when Terry goes to the hospital he and Tim argue and he thumps his son. Later that night, Tim checks out of the hospital and disappears leaving a brief note for his parents. They search frantically for him.

A year goes by… Terry goes on the road to find his son while Molly appears in the show. At a benefit show Katy effects a reconciliation between her mother and Vicky. Father Steve turns up prior to being posted overseas. As Molly performs the film's title song Tim, now a sailor, turns up and so does Terry. The Five Donahues re-form for one night only…

Behind The Scenes: Marilyn made the film as 'punishment' for refusing to appear in *Pink Tights*. As an added sop she was offered *The Seven Year Itch*. She was also given her own back-room staff of Natasha Lytess, Hal Schaefer and Jack Cole. Marilyn was ill when shooting began on 29 May 1954 and her running battle with director Walter Lang did nothing to help. Nor did husband Joe DiMaggio who was notoriously jealous and handy with his fists. He visited the set just once.

Did You Know?: George Chakiris, one of the dancers in the *Heat Wave* number, later went on to win an Oscar for *West Side Story* (1961). Look out for the billboard advertising 'Tim & Katie Donahue' before reverting to the accepted spelling when she appears with her mother 'Molly & Katy Donahue.' The film's original writer Lamar Trotti died aged 52 from a coronary before he could complete the script. He received a posthumous Oscar nomination for his contribution. (The film also won Oscar nods for Best Costume Design and Best Music.) The character of Vicky Parker did not appear in the original story. Because of her exclusive contract with RCA, the voice on the soundtrack belongs to Dolores Gray, not Marilyn. Filming overran so Marilyn went straight into making *The Seven Year Itch* without a break.

What The Critics Say: 'What they like, they repeat. Mr O'Connor does a drink scene early in the film – you know, kid coming home with a snoot-full to shock his parents. A comedy routine. So they do it all again when Mr O'Connor thinks he has been jilted by Marilyn Monroe, a blond [*sic*], baby-faced nightclub singer who complicates the uneven tenor of the family's way… When it comes to spreading talent, Miss Gaynor has the jump on Miss Monroe, whose wriggling and squirming to *Heat Wave* and *Lazy* are embarrassing to behold' Bosley Crowther, *The New York Times*. '*There's No Business Like Showbusiness* is full to overflowing with entertainment material… Photographed in DeLuxe Color, it is a star-studded production with an Irving Berlin score that gives the film rhythm, bounce and a pleasant nostalgic quality… Marilyn stars in three speciality numbers amusingly, as she does a comic burlesque of the sexy singer of naughty songs' Kate Cameron, *New York Daily News*.

The Verdict: Basically, an excuse for lavish production numbers for Irving Berlin songs – and what is wrong with that? 3/5

The Seven Year Itch
(20th Century-Fox, 3 June 1955)

The Crew: Director Billy Wilder. Writers Billy Wilder & George Axelrod. Play George Axelrod. Producers Charles K Feldman & Billy Wilder. Cinematographer Milton R Krasner, ASC. Music Alfred Newman. Sound E Clayton Ward & Harry M Leonard. Art Direction Lyle Wheeler & George W Davis. Set Decoration Walter M Scott & Stuart A Reiss. Special Photographic Effects Ray Kellogg. Editor Hugh S Fowler. Wardrobe Direction Charles LeMaire. Costumes Travilla. Title Designer Saul Bass. Make-Up Ben Nye. Assistant Director Joseph E Richards. Hairstyles Helen Turpin. Subway Effects Saul Wurtzel. Technicolor Colour Consultant Leonard Doss. Associate Producer Doane Harrison. Miss Monroe's Make-Up Allan 'Whitey' Snyder.

The Cast: Marilyn Monroe (The Girl), Tom Ewell (Richard Sherman), Evelyn Keyes (Helen Sherman), Sonny Tufts (Tom MacKenzie), Robert Strauss (Mr Kruhulik the janitor), Oskar Homolka (Dr Brubaker), Marguerite Chapman (Miss Morris the secretary), Donald MacBride (Mr Brady), Butch Bernard (Ricky Sherman), 105 minutes.

The Story: This film has probably the most illegible opening titles I have ever seen. Anyway, New York: Manhattan men send their wives and children away from the sweltering summer heat of the city. Book editor Richard Sherman is no different and packs wife Helen and son Ricky to Algonquin, Maine. 38-year-old (39 in August) Sherman returns to work at Brady & Co (Publishers) with a determination to work hard, not smoke, not drink and definitely no dilly-dallying while his wife is away. He gets off to a good start with a meal at a vegetarian restaurant (260 calories) before going home to his pleasant home, a house divided into three apartments (situated at 164 East 61st Street). The other tenants are the Kaufmans and two interior decorators. As he relaxes with a new manuscript the doorbell rings and when he buzzes it to open a stunning girl is standing there. She has forgotten her front door key and he has to open the door again when the cord of her electric fan gets caught in the door. She tells him she has sublet the Kaufmans' for the summer.

Sherman settles down again with his work to await his wife's 10 o'clock call and reminisces on his 7 years of mostly happy but boring marriage. He allows his imagination to run riot. He lays on a sun lounger on the terrace and the second he moves a tomato plant comes crashing down barely missing him. He shouts upwards in anger only to mellow when he realises it comes from The Girl's apartment and she is naked. He invites her down for a drink and she tells him she will be down as soon as she gets her undies out of the fridge. Apparently, she keeps them in there in the warm weather. As he awaits her arrival his imagination again runs riot. The 22-year-old Girl comes from Denver, Colorado, but it seems a lot of the incidents in her life mirror those in Marilyn's. Strange that. The Girl goes to fetch some champagne and crisps and also changes into something more elegant. The Girl is pleased to discover Sherman is married because every man she meets falls in love with her and proposes. At least, Sherman can't do that. He puts Rachmaninov's *2nd Piano Concerto* on the record player – the girl knows it is classical music "because there's no vocal." She asks him to play the piano and he serenades her with *Chopsticks*. She joins him at the stool but when he attempts to snog her they fall off the stool. Mortified at what he has tried to do, Sherman sends her back to her apartment.

The next day Sherman asks his boss for a fortnight off to stay with his wife and son but Brady denies his request and suggests they hit the town as footloose bachelors - Mrs Brady and the rest of the Brady bunch are in Nantucket. Back in his office Sherman continues to work on the new manuscript which is a treatise on middle-aged men and their straying especially after 7 years of marriage. Brubaker's co-author labels it 'The Seven Year Itch.' Eaten up with guilt and convinced Helen must already know about his 'fling' he calls her long distance only to find she is out on a hayride. His paranoia kicks in and he reckons she is seeing his friend Tom MacKenzie and he asks The Girl out. They go to the pictures to see *The Creature From The Black Lagoon* and The Girl expresses her sympathy for the creature. Walking out The Girl stands on a subway grille as a train passes and her skirt is blown up. They kiss – to prove that the toothpaste she advertises on telly does work and leaves her breath fresh, natch. They return to his apartment because hers doesn't have air-conditioning. She has a TV show to do the next day and asks if she can sleep over because she just knows she won't get any sleep in her own place because of the heat. Then the janitor arrives and spots The Girl's bare leg retrieving her sandals. He gets hold of the right end of the stick and Sherman kicks her out. Sherman's apartment used to be connected to the one upstairs by a staircase but it has been boarded up. The Girl removes the board and sneaks downstairs, and ends up sleeping in the marital bed while Sherman kips on the couch. When he awakens his imagination again runs overtime. He and The Girl kiss again before Tom MacKenzie turns up to fetch the paddle that Ricky had left behind. Sherman accuses MacKenzie of what has happened in his imagination, much to McKenzie's amazement. Then Sherman tells him that for all he cares he (Sherman) could have Marilyn Monroe in his kitchen (He does! He does!) and then knocks the much bigger man out. Sherman sets off for the country with his son's paddle leaving The Girl with the two apartments.

Behind The Scenes: Marilyn had married baseball hero Joe DiMaggio 7 months before filming began. The marriage was already in trouble due to his jealousy and readiness with his fists. At 1am on 15 September 1954 the crew filmed the famous skirt blowing scene at the Trans-Lux Theater on Lexington Avenue and 52nd Street. Fifteen times Marilyn's dress blew into the air and fifteen times the huge crowd (estimated at between 1,000 and 5,000 people) cheered. Joe DiMaggio watched the proceedings with his friend Walter Winchell before storming off, his hands thrust deep into his pockets. Although

Marilyn wore two pairs of knickers her friend Jim Haspiel says her pubes were clearly visible. However, in the end the scenes shot that night were not useable in the film and what finally appears was shot on a Fox soundstage. Following the shoot Marilyn returned to suite 1105-6 of the St Regis Hotel, 2 East 55th Street & 5th Avenue, where she was staying with DiMaggio. They had a violent fight that night and the next day he flew back to California alone. On 5 October 1954 Marilyn announced their separation. They were divorced 22 days later. DiMaggio was back by her side for the première on her 29th birthday in 1955. "We're just good friends," said Marilyn to ward off press speculation of a reconciliation.

Did You Know?: *The Seven Year Itch* was the last film to be made by Marilyn under her original Fox contract, the one she bridled against so much. Filming began on 10 August 1954, immediately after Marilyn had finished *There's No Business Like Showbusiness*. The film ran 13 days over schedule and 10 per cent over budget due in no small part to Marilyn's illness - she caught a serious lung illness while filming the skirt scene on Lexington Avenue. Marilyn filmed her final scenes on 9 January 1955, after she had been suspended by Fox for walking out on her contract. The film has a different ending to the play where The Girl and Sherman consummate their passion. Fox publicised the film by hanging an enormous (52 ft high) poster of Marilyn at Loew's State Theater in Time Square on Broadway at a cost of $1,500. It had to be replaced by a more circumspect version after complaints. Marilyn was nominated for a BAFTA for her performance. Tom Ewell played the rôle of Sherman in the original Broadway production.

What The Critics Say: 'This is the film that every red-blooded American male has been awaiting ever since the publication of the tease photos showing the wind lifting Marilyn Monroe's skirt above her shapely gams. It was worth waiting for. *The Seven Year Itch* is another example of cinema ingenuity in transplanting a stage success to celluloid... Tom Ewell, who reaped critical acclaim in the legit show and won over other contenders for the rôle in the movie, and La Monroe deserve most of the credit for carrying off the comedy coup... her pouting delivery, puckered lips – the personification of this decade's glamour – make her one of Hollywood's top attractions, which she again proves as the not-too-bright model' Philip Strassberg, *New York Daily Mirror*. 'Miss Monroe brings a special personality and a certain physical something or other to the film... From the moment she steps into the picture, in a garment that drapes her shapely form as though she had been skilfully poured into it, the famous screen star with the silver-blonde tresses and the ingenuously wide-eyed stare emanates one suggestion. And that suggestion rather dominates the film. It is – well, why define it? Miss Monroe clearly plays the title rôle. Mr Wilder has permitted Miss Monroe, in her skin-fitting dresses and her frank gyrations, to overpower Mr Ewell. She, without any real dimensions, is the focus of attention in the film' Bosley Crowther, *The New York Times*.

The Verdict: Although this is rated as one of Monroe's best films I found Sherman's paranoid imagination irritating and it certainly put me off. Marilyn is obviously playing herself which is no bad thing but it doesn't save the film in my opinion. 1/5

5. Vulnerable: A Tenderness That Is Affecting

Bus Stop
(20th Century-Fox, 31 August 1956)

The Crew: Director Joshua Logan. Writer George Axelrod. Play Willian Inge. The Four Lads sing *The Bus Stop Song*. Music Alfred Newman & Cyril J Mockridge. Conductor Alfred Newman. Cinematographer Milton Krasner, ASC. Art Direction Lyle R Wheeler & Mark-Lee Kirk. Set Decoration Walter M Scott & Paul S Scott. Special Photographic Effects Ray Kellogg. Editor William Reynolds, ACE. Executive Wardrobe Designer Charles LeMaire. Costumes Travilla. Vocal Supervision Ken Darby. Orchestration Edward B Powell. Assistant Director Ben Kadish. Make-Up Ben Nye. Hairstyles Helen Turpin, CHS. Sound Alfred Bruzlin & Harry M Leonard. Technicolor Colour Consultant Leonard Doss.

The Cast: Marilyn Monroe (Cherie), Don Murray (Beauregard 'Bo' Decker), Arthur O'Connell (Virgil 'Virge' Blessing), Betty Field (Grace), Eileen Heckart (Vera), Robert Bray (Carl), Hope Lange (Elma Duckworth), Hans Conried (Photographer), Casey Adams (Life Reporter), Henry Slate (Nightclub manager), 96 minutes.

The Story: 21-year-old Bo Decker, a gauche, none-too-bright cowboy from Timberhills, Montana, is on his way to Phoenix, Arizona, to compete in the rodeo. Accompanying him is his old friend Virgil who suggests it might be time for Bo to find himself a girl. Bo says he wants an angel but Virgil suggests a homely girl with an accommodating nature might be more up Bo's street.

Across the road from their hotel is the Blue Dragon saloon and while Bo finishes his shower and bath (yes, both) Virgil makes his way across to the establishment. The 'chantoose' there is Cherie, a girl from the Ozarks who wants to go to Hollywood & Vine, be discovered and become a star. The one thing holding her back is her lack of talent but she doesn't see that as a handicap. She makes her way to Virgil's table and persuades him to buy her a whisky at 60¢ a time. After four whiskys she is still stone cold sober and he becomes suspicious – rightly so because she is drinking tea. Before he can protest further at the scam, she is hustled away to sing *That Old Black Magic* on stage – badly. As she goes through her routine Bo bursts through the doors of the saloon and falls madly in love at first sight with Cherie. He jumps on a table to tell the audience to be quiet so Cherie can sing in peace. When she is done, he follows her off stage and professes his love for her. He takes her outside and he coyly tells her what his name Beauregard means – "good looking." He constantly mispronounces her name as Cherry. She says she is attracted to him and they kiss.

Back inside he tells Virgil they are engaged to be married, much to Cherie's horror and Virgil's amazement. Bo tells Virgil Cherie is physically attracted to him but Virgil points out that may not be enough. "What else is there?" asks Bo. "Intellectual attraction, poetry and the like." Bo says he doesn't know poetry, but can read and write and recite the Gettsyburg Address! What a catch!

At 9am the next morning he bursts into her room only to find her fast asleep since she hadn't got to bed until 5am. She tells him she has no intention of going to no stupid rodeo, no intention of marrying him. To show his 'intellectual' capability Bo recites the Gettsyburg Address! Bo is not one to take a simple no for an answer and drags Cherie to the parade hoisting her on his shoulder so she can get a better look. Despite professing ambivalence towards him Cherie can't bring herself to look when he gets on the bucking bronco. She shows her friend Vera the $43 engagement ring Bo has bought her. After each round Bo shouts to Cherie much to her embarrassment. She tells Vera she can't get married anyway because no arrangements have been made. Then she spots a clergyman and makes a dash for freedom across the arena.

Back in her room, Cherie packs her case and takes it to the saloon in case she has to make a rapid exit. In the saloon Virgil tells Cherie that he doesn't want her to marry Bo either. Then the man of the moment comes in clutching $4,000 he has won by triumphing in each rodeo discipline except one, the steer wrestling. His brashness appals Cherie and she runs to her dressing room making a bid for freedom through the window. She runs to the bus depot hotly pursued by Bo and Virgil and buys a one-way ticket to Los Angeles. Bo lassos Cherie and the next thing she knows, she is on the bus to Montana still clad in her stage costume.

Cherie enlists the help of fellow passenger Elma Duckworth to help her change. As she does so the driver, Carl, looks in his rear-view mirror and almost crashes the bus awaking Bo. The weather worsens and the vehicle has to make an overnight stop at Grace's Diner. Bo and Virgil have again fallen asleep on the bus and awakening Bo goes into the diner, sees Cherie's suitcase inside and is furious. He lifts Cherie and decides to take her to the nearest preacher but is stopped by Virgil and Carl. The three go outside and Virgil tries to knock some sense into Bo allowing Carl to successfully finish the fight for him. Bo doesn't know that Carl used to be a wrestling champion.

By the next day the snow has cleared and a route for the bus has been cleared by a snowplough. At Virgil's insistence Bo apologises for his behaviour, returns Cherie's scarf which he wore for luck in the rodeo, but refuses to take back the ring he gave her. Virgil goes to help Carl fit the snowchains to the bus and Cherie takes the opportunity to chat to Bo. She tells him that she had "quite a few" boyfriends in the past. He isn't deterred and tells Cherie he is still a virgin. Carl returns and offers Bo the hand of friendship which he begrudgingly accepts. Bo asks Cherie if he can kiss her goodbye and they snog properly before Bo runs away. He comes back for one last try: "I like you the way you are, so how do I care how you got that way." Cherie is impressed and Bo tells Cherie he wishes she was going back to the ranch with him. "I'd go anywhere in the world with you now, anywhere at all," she replies. Timberhills, Montana, is a start I suppose…

Behind The Scenes: The change in location from Phoenix to Sun Valley, Idaho, affected Marilyn's weak constitution and she came down with a nasty case of bronchitis necessitating closure of the set. Marilyn didn't make any friends on set apart from Eileen Heckart who played her on-screen best friend. Marilyn was given gorgeous outfits for her rôle as Cherie but she was more concerned with professionalism than looking good and she took costumier Billy Travilla to the wardrobe department where she picked out a number of threadbare outfits more suitable to Cherie. Marilyn was dating Arthur Miller but still saw other men and one day a man on location asked her out. She accepted but lost her temper with her new PR Pat Newcombe when the man arrived to collect Marilyn and found Newcombe in a state of undress. (Both women were happy to wander around their respective suites in their smalls.) Newcombe was history… for now.

Did You Know?: Under her new contract Marilyn could choose her own director and plumped for John Huston but he was unable to work because of other commitments so her second choice was Josh Logan. This was the first film for which Paula Strasberg acted as Marilyn's coach at $1,500 a week. The film is unavailable on tape in America owing to legal wrangles with the estate of William Lange. Don Murray was nominated for both an Oscar and a BAFTA. Marilyn felt she was cheated out of an Oscar nomination by director Logan who cut much of Cherie's moving monologue with Hope Lange on the bus.

What The Critics Say: 'This is Marilyn's show, and, my friend, she shows plenty in figure, beauty and talent. The girl is a terrific comedi-

enne as the bewildered little "chantoose" of the honky-tonk circuit. Her
stint at the Actor's Studio in New York certainly didn't hurt our girl'
Dorothy Manners, *Los Angeles Examiner*. 'Hold on to your chairs,
everybody, and get set for a rattling surprise. Marilyn Monroe has
finally proved herself an actress in *Bus Stop*. She and the picture are
swell!... For the striking fact is that Mr Logan has got her to do a great
deal more than wiggle and pout and pop her big eyes and play the syn-
thetic vamp in this film. He has got her to be the beat-up B-girl of Mr
Inge's play, even down to the Ozark accent and the look of pellagra
about her skin. He has got her to be the tinselled floosie, the semi-
moronic doll who is found in a Phoenix clip joint by a cowboy of
equally limited brains and is hotly pursued by this suitor to a snow-
bound bus stop in the Arizona wilds. And, what's more important, he
has got her to light the small flame of dignity that splutters pathetically
in this chippie and to make a rather moving sort of her. Fortunately for
her and for the tradition of diligence leading to success, she gives a
performance in this picture that marks her as a genuine acting star, not
just a plushy personality and a sex symbol, as she has previously been'
Bosley Crowther, *The New York Times*.

The Verdict: Richard Sherman was irritating in *The Seven Year Itch*
and Bo Decker is loud, thick and gauche. The Girl in *Itch* was delightful and Cherie is also wonderful and so this time she saves the film. 4/5

The Prince And The Showgirl
(Marilyn Monroe Productions, 13 June 1957)

The Crew: Director/Producer Laurence Olivier. Writer & Play *The Sleeping
Prince* Terence Rattigan. Executive Producer Milton Greene. Executive In Charge
Of Production Hugh Perceval. Associate Director Anthony Bushell. First Assistant
Director David Orton. Cinematographer Jack Cardiff. Production Designer Roger
Furse. Production Manager Teddy Joseph. Art Direction Carmen Dillon. Editor
Jack Harris. Sound John Mitchell & Gordon McCallum. Ladies' Costumes Beatrice
Dawson. Make-Up Toni Sforzini. Hairdresser Gordon Bond. Set Decoration Dario
Simoni. Music Richard Addinsell. Choreographer William Chapel.

The Cast: Richard Wattis (Northbrooke), David Horne (Foreign Office Minister),
Jeremy Spenser (King Nicholas of Carpathia), Sybil Thorndike (Queen Dowager),
Laurence Olivier (Grand Duke Charles, Regent of Carpathia), Harold Goodwin
(Call Boy), Gladys Henson (Dresser), Marilyn Monroe (Elsie Marina), Jean Kent
(Masie Springfield), Charles Victor (Theatre Manager), Daphne Anderson (Fanny),
Vera Day (Betty), Gillian Owen (Maggie), Esmond Knight (Colonel Hoffman), Paul
Hardwick (Major Domo), Dennis Edwards (Valet), Andrea Melandrinos (Valet),
Rosamund Greenwood & Margot Lister (Ladies-In-Waiting), 117 minutes.

The Story: London, 1911: The whole of the capital is awash with
foreign dignitaries in town for the coronation of King George V. The

Regent of Carpathia spots an American entertainer, Elsie Marina, in a show and falls for her. He invites her back to the Carpathian Embassy for dinner and, he hopes, more but Elsie is a moral girl as girls were in 1911. A problem arises when Nicholas decides he wants to ascend the throne immediately rather than when he attains his majority in a year and a half.

Behind The Scenes: On 9 February 1956 Marilyn and Laurence Olivier held a press conference at the Plaza Hotel, 768 5th Avenue, New York, to announce the making of the movie and the spaghetti strap on Marilyn's dress broke. Marilyn insisted it was an accident but Olivier was convinced she had done it deliberately to upstage him. It set the tone for the production. Marilyn married Arthur Miller in June 1956 (following his political troubles in America) and on 14 July flew to England where they stayed at Parkside House, Englefield Green, Egham, Surrey, for four months during filming. The movie was shot (from 7 August until 17 November 1956) at Pinewood Studios. Before one take Olivier foolishly said: "Okay, Marilyn, be sexy." Marilyn was understandably furious especially as she was, nominally, Olivier's boss. The knight didn't appreciate Paula Strasberg's presence on set. On 29 October Marilyn was presented to the Queen at the Empire Theatre, Leicester Square after the Royal Command Performance presentation of *The Battle Of The River Plate*.

Did You Know?: This was the only film ever made by Marilyn Monroe Productions. The movie needed just two days of retakes and came in under budget. Marilyn referred to Olivier as "Mister Sir." She received a bonus of $160,000 being 10% of the profits.

What The Critics Say: 'We are all bound to tell you that Miss Monroe never gets out of that dress and Mr Rattigan never swings out of the circle in which he has permitted his thin plot to get stuck… He has not let his story do much more than go around and around, and then come to a sad end' Bosley Crowther, *The New York Times*. 'Marilyn Monroe has never seemed more in command of herself as a person and comedienne. She manages to make laughs without sacrificing the real Marilyn to play-acting. This, of course, is something one can expect from great, talented and practised performers. It comes as a most pleasant surprise from Marilyn Monroe, who has been half-actress, half-sensation' Archer Winsten, *New York Post*.

The Verdict: One of Marilyn's best performances. 3/5

Some Like It Hot
(United Artists, 29 March 1959)

The Crew: Producer/Director Billy Wilder. Writers Billy Wilder & IAL Diamond. Story Robert Thoeren & M Logan. Cinematographer Charles Lang, Jr, ASC. Associate Producers Doane Harrison & IAL Diamond. Miss Monroe's Gowns Orry-Kelly. Background score Adolph Deutsch. Songs Supervisor Matty Malneck. Art Director Ted Haworth. Set Decoration Edward G Boyle. Property Tom Plews. Special Photographic Effects Milt Rice. Editor Arthur P Schmidt. Script Continuity John Franco. Make-up Emile LaVigne, SMA. Hair Styles Alice Monte & Agnes Flanagan. Production Manager Allen K Wood. Assistant Director Sam Nelson. Wardrobe Bert Hendrikson. Music Editor Eve Newman. Sound Fred Lau.

The Cast: Marilyn Monroe (Sugar Kane *née* Kovalchick), Tony Curtis (Joe/Josephine), Jack Lemmon (Jerry/Daphne), George Raft (Spats Colombo), Pat O'Brien (Mulligan), Joe E Brown (Osgood E Fielding, III), Nehemiah Persoff (Little Bonaparte), Joan Shawlee (Sweet Sue), Billy Gray (Sig Poliakoff), George E Stone (Toothpick Charlie), Dave Barry (Beinstock), Mike Mazurki (Spat's henchman), Edward G Robinson, Jr (Paradise), 122 minutes.

The Story: Chicago, 1929. Two perennially broke musicians, Jerry and Joe, land their first job in months. Unfortunately, it's in a speakeasy run by gangster Spats Colombo. The place is raided by the police but Jerry and Joe make good their escape. Their agent, Sig Poliakoff, has just two jobs — one in an all-girl band bound for Florida and one gig 100 miles north but they have no car to get there. Joe sweet-talks Poliakoff's secretary, Nellie, into lending them her car for the gig but when they go to collect it from the Clark Street garage they accidentally witness the St Valentine's Day Massacre. With no other option they disguise themselves as women (Daphne and Josephine), and hide in a touring all-girl band: Sweet Sue and her Society Syncopators. The gangsters are determined to catch up with them. Meanwhile, they befriend the band's singer and ukulele player Sugar Kane (*née* Kovalchick) who is a sweet if dizzy girl with a drink problem. Sweet Sue has threatened to sack Sugar if she catches her with alcohol.

On the train the band are practising *Running Wild* when Sugar accidentally drops a bottle of bourbon but before she can be sacked Daphne says the booze is hers. Later that night Sugar climbs into Daphne's bunk to thank her for covering for her and soon all the girls except Josephine are having a party. Daphne gets the hiccups and the girls shove ice down her back. Fearing her cover is about to be blown, she pulls the emergency brake. Arriving in Miami, they settle into the Seminole-Ritz Hotel and begin to enjoy the sun.

While Daphne goes swimming with the girls Joe dons the clothes he has stolen from the band's touring manager, Beinstock, and impersonates a young, impotent, oil millionaire with a Cary Grant accent. (By all accounts, Grant loved the impression.) Meanwhile, Daphne is wooed by a real eccentric millionaire Osgood Fielding III who has been married "seven or eight times... Mama is keeping score" and becomes engaged. He gives her a diamond bracelet as an engagement present while Joe utilises Osgood's yacht to seduce Sugar. In fact, she seduces him after she swallows his line about his impotence.

Just as things seem to be going smoothly, the hotel hosts the 10th annual convention of the Friends of Italian Opera, in reality the Mafia. Spats and his henchmen get in the same lift as Daphne and Josephine and make a play for them. Back in their rooms they decide to make a run for it. Having told her he has to marry the daughter of a Venezuelan oil magnate, Joe doesn't want to hurt Sugar so he gives her Osgood's bracelet as a going away present. As the pair make their escape they are spotted by Spats' goons who give chase. Giving them the slip, Joe and Jerry hide under a table in the banqueting hall just as the mob enter for their dinner. Spats and his mob are gunned down and Joe and Jerry escape in the mêlée as the police burst in.

Once again donning drag, Daphne calls Osgood. Josephine hears Sugar sing *I'm Through With Love* and heartbroken reveals his true identity to her. The sight of two 'women' kissing not surprisingly arouses suspicions and Josephine's cover is blown. Daphne and Josephine make a dash for the pier to meet Osgood only for Sugar to chase after them. On the speedboat taking them to Osgood's yacht Daphne confesses 'her' secret to which Osgood responds with the immortal line, "Well, nobody's perfect!"

Behind The Scenes: In October 1958, by which time most of the strenuous shots had been filmed, Marilyn found herself pregnant again. Heartbreak was to follow as she miscarried the child on 16 December in her third month.

Did You Know?: Marilyn could not sit down between takes because her costumes were tight fitting, so she had to rest standing up in what looked like an upright barber's chair. Curtis and Lemmon had their legs and chests shaved and a female impersonator called Barbette was brought onto the set to show them how women behave, carry themselves, etc. However, Barbette walked off because he did not get on with Jack Lemmon. The working title for the film was *Not Tonight, Josephine!* Although director Billy Wilder's original choices to play the musicians were Tony Curtis and Jack Lemmon, United Artists wanted Frank Sinatra to play Jerry/Daphne. The choice for Sugar was

Mitzi Gaynor. Sinatra agreed to play the rôle but then failed to keep an appointment to discuss the part and no more was heard from Ol' Blue Eyes. By this time with Monroe on board UA didn't much mind who was cast as Jerry/Daphne. Enter Jack Lemmon. To test out the authenticity of their make-up and costumes Lemmon and Curtis visited the ladies' room in drag and not one of the women in there batted an eyelid. Having their outfits retouched they carried out the experiment again. One of the other patrons immediately said, "Hi, Tony." Tony Curtis based his portrayal in the film on Grace Kelly, ZaSu Pitts and his mother. According to screenwriter Henry Ephron, Marilyn would French-kiss Tony Curtis in their scenes to make Arthur Miller jealous. Paradise (Edward G Robinson, Jr), one of Bonaparte's henchmen, stands flipping a coin and is asked by Bonaparte (George Raft) where he picked up that cheap trick. In the film *Scarface* (1932) Raft portrayed a mob heavy whose trademark was to flip a coin. While Marilyn was shooting at the Sam Goldwyn Studio, Arthur Miller used his time trying to persuade Clark Gable to accept the rôle of Gay Langland in *The Misfits*. Eventually, it was the financial lure that persuaded Gable not Miller's rhetoric.

What The Critics Say: 'To coin a phrase, Marilyn has never looked better. She's a comedienne with that combination of sex appeal and timing that just can't be beat' *Variety*. 'As the band's somewhat simple singer-ukulele player, Miss Monroe, whose figure simply cannot be overlooked, contributes more assets than the obvious ones to this madcap romp. As a pushover for gin and the tonic effect of saxophone players, she sings a couple of whispery old numbers (*Running Wild* and *I Wanna Be Loved By You*) and also proves to be the epitome of a dumb blonde and a talented comedienne... *Some Like It Hot* does cool off considerably now and again but Mr Wilder and his carefree clowns keep it crackling and funny most of the time ' A H Weiler, *The New York Times*. 'To get down to cases, Marilyn does herself proud, giving a performance of such intrinsic quality that you begin to believe she's only being herself and it is herself who fits into that distant period and this picture so well' Archer Winsten, *New York Post*.

The Verdict: *Some Like It Hot* is a joy to watch. Funny. lively, chirpy, it hits the right note more often than not. Marilyn is endearing, Lemmon and Curtis a delight and the dialogue fresh. It's a 5/5 all the way.

Let's Make Love
(20th Century-Fox, 8 September 1960)

The Crew: Director George Cukor. Writer Hal Kanter. Additional Material Norman Krasna. Producer Jerry Wald. Music Lionel Newman. Associate Earle H Hagen. Words & Music Sammy Cahn & James Van Heusen. *My Heart Belongs To Daddy* by Cole Porter. Choreographer Jack Cole. Cinematographer Daniel L Fapp, ASC. Main Title & Prologue Designer Gene Allen. Colour Coordination Hoyningen-Huene. Art Direction Lyle R Wheeler & Gene Allen. Set Decoration Walter M Scott & Fred M Maclean. Assistant Director David Hall. Editor David Bretherton. Costumes Dorothy Jeakins. Make-up Ben Nye. Hairstyles Helen Turpin, CRS. Sound W D Flick & Warren B Delapain.

The Cast: Marilyn Monroe (Amanda Dell), Yves Montand (Jean-Marc Clément), Tony Randall (Alexander Coffman), Frankie Vaughan (Tony Danton), Wilfrid Hyde-White (George Wales), David Burns (Oliver Burton), Michael David (Dave Kerry), Mara Lynn (Lily Nyles), Dennis King, Jr (Abe Miller), Joe Besser (Lamont), Milton Berle (Himself), Bing Crosby (Himself), Gene Kelly (Himself), 105 minutes.

The Story: The history of Jean-Marc Clément's family to the present day… Broadway PR turned corporate PR Alexander Coffman spots a small item in *Variety* about a show called *Let's Make Love* in a theatre in the round in Greenwich Village. He brings it to the attention of his boss George Wales who in turn tells his superior and the bloke who owns the company the billionaire Jean-Marc Clément. Coffman suggests Clément attend a rehearsal of the show and as he walks into the theatre blonde bombshell Amanda Dell is performing a sexy version of *My Heart Belongs To Daddy*. He is immediately smitten. Meanwhile, the director mistakes Clément for a lookalike auditioning for the part of the billionaire in the play. Clément is cast as his own double and tells the company his name is Alexander Dumas. Amanda tells Clément/Dumas that she thinks Clément is nothing but a rich louse. Then singer Tony Danton enters pretending to be drunk. Amanda clearly has a soft spot for him. To amuse the company Clément/Dumas tells a joke that his sycophantic sidekicks find hysterical but the reaction from the seen-it-all, heard-it-all company is very different. In his Rolls-Royce on the way back to the office Clément tells Coffman to buy him a new joke for $1,000. He visits Lamont, an old scriptwriting buddy who does his best work in a sauna. Clément also sets his man Wilson a mission to find out everything about Amanda. Besides Danton, she is seeing someone else, a married man. The next day at rehearsals, Lamont turns up and is horrified to hear Clément/Dumas tell 'his' joke. Clément/Dumas tells Amanda he is a jewellery salesman and 'sells' Amanda a $10,000 necklace for $5 only for her to pass it on to another of the cast. Clément/Dumas retrieves the bauble by telling her that it is made from radioactive diamonds. George Wales learns that the theatre is owned indirectly by the Clément organisation and decides to throw some muscle around by demanding a year's rent in advance knowing full well the company won't be able to afford that. Coffman confronts Clément about the plan but he is in the dark as Wales has acted alone. Clément arranges for Wales to become an angel and buy 51% of the show. Following the rehearsal Clément hires Milton Berle to teach him comedy, Bing Crosby to teach him singing and Gene Kelly to coach him in the terpsichorean arts. Danton is angry when Clément/Dumas is handed the best song and threatens to leave the company. Amanda agrees to dinner with Clément/Dumas so Danton can have a crack at performing the song in front of George Wales. Over dinner – for which Amanda offers to go Dutch – Clément/Dumas proposes. They talk of trust and Amanda confesses that the only reason they are dining is so that Danton can have his chance. Clément/Dumas reveals his 'secret' but Amanda makes a sharp exit and runs back to the theatre. There she believes Clément/Dumas is mentally unstable. She tells him money is unimportant to her and he melts. They kiss. She again asks his real identity and is upset when he insists he is Jean-Marc Clément. Angry, the billionaire takes out an injunction to close the show on breach of privacy. Clément/Dumas suggests visiting Clément Enterprises to sort out the matter. Once there Clément/Dumas and Amanda are left alone and he sits at his desk, much to her horror. She still thinks he is nutty. When the truth dawns, she faints. Coming round, she is angry and humiliated. She runs to the lift but he stops it and climbs in…

Behind The Scenes: Although Jean-Marc Clément and Amanda Dell didn't get together until the end of the film off-screen Marilyn and Yves Montand engaged in a passionate affair that really signalled the end of her marriage to Arthur Miller. Miller and Monroe and Montand and his wife, Simone Signoret (1921-1985), stayed in adjoining bungalows at the Beverly Hills Hotel. Miller left to go to New York while Signoret travelled to Rome leaving the way open for their spouses to have a very public affair. In later years Signoret rarely laid much importance on the fling. "If Marilyn is in love with my husband, it proves she has good taste," she said. She also debunked the myth that Montand reportedly said Marilyn "had a schoolgirl crush" on him. His English wasn't good enough to know the idiom. Signoret and Montand stayed married until her death on 30 September 1985.

Did You Know?: Billy Wilder was originally scheduled to direct but was signed to make *The Apartment*. Supposedly Yul Brynner, Cary Grant, Rock Hudson, William Holden, James Stewart, Gregory Peck and Charlton Heston all turned down the rôle of Jean-Marc Clément before Montand accepted it. Arthur Miller was an uncredited contributor to the script "I did what I could... But we were beating a dead horse." The film was hit by an actors' strike six weeks into filming.

What The Critics Say: 'The old Monroe dynamism is lacking in the things she is given to do by the cliché-clogged script of Norman Krasna and by George Cukor, who directed the film. It doesn't seem very important that she is finally brought together with Mr Montand' Bosley Crowther, *The New York Times*. 'In the acting department Miss Monroe is not impressive as in comedy-type rôles. She plays a straight part here and does very little that is effective. Visually? Marilyn offers her famous curves, not a little on the fleshy side. Diet, anyone?' Lowell E Redelings, *Hollywood Citizen News*. 'Marilyn Monroe is geared for some of the loudest laughter of her life *in Let's Make Love*... It is a gay, preposterous and completely delightful romp... Marilyn actually dares comparison with Mary Martin by singing *My Heart Belongs To Daddy* in her first scene. The night I saw it, the audience broke into the picture with applause' Alton Cook, *New York World-Telegram And Sun*.

The Verdict: Usually slated by critics, *Let's Make Love* isn't Marilyn's best film but it isn't half as bad as some would have you believe. Despite Mr Redelings' comments, Marilyn looks gorgeous and if anyone's acting is flawed it is Yves Montand's. A respectable 2/5

The Misfits
(United Artists, 1 February 1961)

The Crew: Director John Huston. Producer Frank E Taylor. Writer Arthur Miller. Music Alex North. Cinematographer Russell Metty, ASC. Art Direction Stephen Grimes & William Newberry. Set Decoration Frank McKelvy. Editor George Tomasini, ACE. Production Manager C O Erickson. Second Unit Director Tom Shaw. Sound Philip Mitchell & Charles Grenzbach. Assistant Director Carl Beringer. Assistant to Mr Taylor Edward Parone. Miss Monroe's Wardrobe Jean Louis. Hair styling Sydney Guilaroff & Agnes Flanagan, CHE. Make-Up Allan Snyder, Frank Prehoda, SMA & Frank LaRue. Wrangler Billy Jones. Stuntman Chuck Robertson. Miss Monroe's Coach Paula Strasberg.

The Cast: Clark Gable (Gay Langland), Marilyn Monroe (Rosalyn Taber), Montgomery Clift (Perce Howland), Thelma Ritter (Isabelle Steers), Eli Wallach (Guido), Kevin McCarthy (Raymond Taber), 124 minutes.

The Story: Housewife Rosalyn Taber, a sexually promiscuous, sophisticated woman who has worked as an occasional dance teacher, goes to stay in Reno, Nevada, to await her divorce from husband, Raymond. She stays at the home of Isabelle Steers, apparently a regular haunt for soon-to-be divorcées — this will be the 77th time Isabelle has witnessed a divorce. Rosalyn's car is full of dents because men deliberately bump into her so they can start a conversation. The car won't start so Guido from Jack's Reno Garage gives them a lift to the courtroom. On the steps of the building Raymond tries to talk her out of the divorce but Rosalyn won't be dissuaded. Guido drives to the station where his friend Gay Langland is seeing off a girlfriend, Susan. She wants him to join her at "the second largest laundry in St Louis" but he refuses. Gay and Guido discuss getting away from it all "where there are no people — male or female."

After her divorce Rosalyn and Isabelle go for a drink at Harrah's Bar where Rosalyn orders a scotch on the rocks. There she pets a dog that belongs to Gay and Guido does the honours. Rosalyn decides to rent a car so she can look round Reno. Guido quits his job and the four of them ride out to his house in the desert. Guido has never really lived in the house and since his wife died has never really wanted to. The foursome settle down for a drink. Guido drives the car up so they can hear the radio, the house having no electricity. Gay and Rosalyn dance before Guido steps in and proves himself well versed at the terpsichorean arts.

Rosalyn gets drunk so Gay drives her home and on the way tries it on with her. She rebuffs him. Collecting her things from Isabelle's, Gay drives Rosalyn's back to Guido's and again tries for a kiss. This time she is more responsive. As a thank you, Gay cooks her breakfast next morning. They spend time together — swimming, riding — getting to know each other. Guido flies his plane over them. Meanwhile, Gay has noticed a rabbit has chewed their lettuce and gets his gun to shoot it. Rosalyn pleads for the animal "I can't see anything killed, Gay." Gay doesn't understand Rosalyn's viewpoint but the argument is aborted when Guido and Isabelle arrive. Guido is given a guided tour of his house and in one room the inside of a closet is decorated with pictures of Marilyn Monroe! Rosalyn quickly shuts the door saying Gay put them up for a joke but Guido wants a closer look.

When they sit down for drinks, Guido asks Gay if he would be interested in mustanging. They need a third man and set off for the Dayton

70

rodeo. On the way they encounter Perce Howland who has worked with Guido and Gay before. Giving him a lift, they ask Perce if he would be interested in joining them. In a bar Rosalyn raises $145 with her proficiency with a biff-a-bat. A drunken cowboy gropes Rosalyn's backside almost causing a punch-up with Guido. As they leave the bar Gay proposes but Rosalyn tells him he doesn't have to marry her. A churchgoing lady persuades Rosalyn to hand over a good part of her money before Gay stops her "She hasn't sinned that much."

Isabelle sees her ex-husband with his new wife, Clara, her old friend and invites them to stay at her house. Rosalyn can't watch the rodeo especially when Perce is thrown by his mount. Rosalyn is amazed when Perce announces he wants to ride a bull and offers him the money from the bar if he doesn't do it. Perce is determined but is thrown again and it is only Gay's quick thinking that stops him being trampled by the bull. Rosalyn sits in the car crying her eyes out. Gay tries to explain and suggests they go for a drink in a local saloon. Perce dances with Rosalyn much to the frustration of Guido who hasn't got over her getting off with his friend and is still carrying a torch for her. Perce feels queer and goes outside with Rosalyn where he spills his heart out to her. A drunken Gay comes out to find them and to intro-duce Rosalyn to his children. When they return to the bar the Langland kids have done a disappearing act, embarrassed by their drunken father. Gay climbs atop a car to see if he can spot them but falls and knocks himself unconscious.

A drunken Guido drives Rosalyn and the comatose Gay home very quickly scaring Rosalyn. Back at the house Rosalyn tells Gay she is scared he doesn't like her anymore. "Oh Gay, love me, love me." The next day the four of them travel up to the mountains and it is there that Rosalyn finally realises that the three men intend to sell the mustangs they capture for pet food. Upset, she believed they would be used by children for riding. Her opinion of Gay changes but he tells her that some people would look down at her for what she has done but not him. They are friends again. Guido offers to fly Rosalyn home.

Next day the mustanging begins in earnest. Guido flies off in search of the horses and finds six —a stallion, four mares and a colt — not the fifteen they were expecting. Guido lands and they chase the horses in the truck, lassoing them with tires attached to ropes to slow them down. Rosalyn can hardly bear to look. As the three try to tame the stallion Rosalyn runs to Gay and begs him to let the horses go. He

71

refuses and brings the horse down. As he stands over the creature he ponders giving the horse to Rosalyn but then she offers him $200 and his pride is hurt and he refuses. She tells him she didn't intend to insult him. They all get into the truck — Gay and Perce in the back. Rosalyn is sitting next to Guido in the front and he makes yet another play for her. Rosalyn isn't impressed by his fine words accusing him of feeling sorry only for himself. They come across another horse, a 15-year-old mare, but Perce doesn't join in with the roping. Gay and Guido work out they will make between $110 and $120 but Perce rejects the money. He only came along for the ride he says. Rosalyn has had enough and screams at them calling them murderers. Guido tells Gay what they can do without her but Gay tells him to be quiet. Perce's conscience is bothering him and he asks Rosalyn if she wants him to set the horses free. She says no but the two of them set off in the truck and Perce releases the horses, much to Rosalyn's obvious delight. Gay chases after one and catching the rope is dragged behind the horse and fights it until the horse is exhausted. (A stuntman's face was smashed by the horse's hooves during filming to Gable's annoyance. The stuntman had escaped injury on the first two takes but John Huston insisted on a third and the injury occurred then. Gable thought Huston had a touch of the sadist about him.) While Guido congratulates him, Gay lets the horse go. He tells Perce to let the mare go and offers to drive Rosalyn home.

Behind The Scenes: Marilyn's marriage to Arthur Miller was falling apart and a week after the film wrapped the couple announced they would divorce. On set Arthur Miller met and fell in love with divorced Magnum agency photographer Ingeborg Morath. They married on 7 February 1962 and had a daughter, Rebecca Augusta, on 15 September 1962, a month after Marilyn's death. Rebecca, herself an actress, is married to the actor Daniel Day-Lewis. Filming was a very unhappy experience for Marilyn. "It's their movie," she once moaned. "It's really about the cowboys and the horses. That's all they need. They don't need me at all. Not to act — just for the money. To put my name on the marquee." A book was published in New York in 1995 by The Vestal Press entitled *I Remember Marilyn*. Written by g Peter Collins, it purports to tell the story of a sixteen-month love affair between Collins, eight years younger, and Marilyn. They supposedly met in September 1959 shortly after Marilyn had finished filming *Some Like It Hot*. Collins claims to have rescued her from a suicide attempt in room

631 at the Berkeley Hotel. She also allegedly rang him from Reno while filming *The Misfits* asking him to visit her. Collins says Marilyn sent him a letter signing off "I love you very much. Your Marilyn" but decides not to publish the document. He does, however, publish a picture he claims is the only one of him with Marilyn. Conveniently, they had a 'no photos' clause in their relationship. Collins has his back to the camera. He reports that after a night with Marilyn her mascara stained his shirt, so he was given one belonging to Montgomery Clift. In a rather far-fetched tale that stretches credulity to its limits, he was somehow given the picture by the grandson of the woman who took it. How he was tracked down 30 years later is not explained nor is his uncanny resemblance to Montgomery Clift and the 'coincidence' that he was given Clift's shirt, one identical to the one the actor wears in nearly all the publicity stills taken during the filming.

Did You Know?: In one scene 32 minutes into the film Rosalyn is laying naked in bed when Gay comes into the room and kisses her. As she sits up, her bare breast is revealed. Director Huston cut the scene in the final edit. United Artists were unhappy with the finished version of the film and producer Taylor, director Huston and writer Miller all agreed to reshoot a number of scenes. However, Clark Gable's contract stipulated that he had script approval and he refused to consider the idea. Today's stars are escorted by enormous retinues that add costs to the production of a film. Marilyn had quite a sizeable entourage consisting of a press agent, coach Paula Strasberg, hairdressers Sydney Guilaroff and Agnes Flanagan, make-up artist Allan 'Whitey' Snyder, her friend Bunny Gardel, her stand-in Evelyn Moriarty, masseur Ralph Roberts, plus a secretary, wardrobe assistant, seamstress, chauffeur and maid Hazel Washington. Just before her first scene with Clark Gable, her childhood idol, Marilyn psyched herself up by taking a deep breath and saying, "Rhett Butler, to think I'm working with him." One scene, half an hour or so into the film, called for Rosalyn to eat eggs that Gay has prepared for her. Before John Huston had the shot he wanted in the can Marilyn had chomped her way through two dozen eggs. On another occasion Marilyn, relaxing in her caravan dressing room, was introduced to the producer of a promotional trailer for the film and greeted him with the words, "Am I glad to see you. The air-conditioning doesn't work in here." Clark Gable was paid $750,000 for his work on the film plus 10% of the gross profits and $48,000 per week overtime. Marilyn and John Huston trousered $300,000 each while Arthur

Miller received $225,000. The crew's nickname for Paula Strasberg was 'Black Bart' because she always wore black clothes. The scene where Marilyn plays with a biff-a-bat was written by Arthur Miller after he saw her playing with one one day on location.

What The Critics Say: 'After a long drought of vital American pictures one can now cheer, for *The Misfits* is so distinctly American nobody but an American could have made it. To be honest, I'm not sure anybody could have made it except John Huston from an original script by Arthur Miller, and it is hard to believe Miller could have written it without Marilyn Monroe. There are lines one feels Miss Monroe must have said on her own… Here Miss Monroe is magic, but not a living pin-up dangled in skintight satin before our eyes… And can anyone deny that in this film these performers are at their best? You forget they are performing and feel that they "are"' Paul V Beckley, *New York Herald Tribune*. 'As the fancy-free divorcée who takes up with [a] footloose mustang wrangler, Marilyn plays a rôle into which are written bits and pieces reminiscent of her own life. The wrangler is all uncomplicated masculinity, virile, violent and, in spirit, the perfect part for Clark Gable' *Life*. 'Gable has never done anything better on the screen, nor has Miss Monroe. Gable's acting is vibrant and lusty, hers true to the character as written by Miller… It is a poignant conflict between a man and a woman in love, with each trying to maintain individual characteristics and preserve a fundamental way of life' Kate Cameron, *New York Daily News*. 'Miss Monroe has seldom looked worse; the camera is unfailingly unflattering. But there is a delicacy about her playing, and a tenderness that is affecting' *The Hollywood Reporter*.

The Verdict: Viewed today *The Misfits* is a sombre film with very little evocation of passion or emotion. The undoubtedly fine cast fail to shine. This is due in no small part to the problems they all faced but still the film is ultimately disappointing. It is remembered mainly because it was the last completed films of Marilyn Monroe and Clark Gable. 2/5

Something's Got To Give
(20th Century-Fox, uncompleted 1962)

The Crew: Director George Cukor. Writers Walter Bernstein & Nunnally Johnson. Play Samuel & Bella Spewack. Producer Henry T Weinstein. Editor David Bretherton. Associate Producer/Art Director Gene Allen. Costumer Marjorie Plecher. Make-Up Allan 'Whitey' Snyder. Assistant Director Buck Hall. Costumes Jean-Louis.

The Cast: Marilyn Monroe (Ellen Arden), Dean Martin (Nick Arden), Cyd Charisse (Bianca), Wally Cox (Adam), Phil Silvers (Insurance Salesman), Tom Tryon (Stephen Burkett), Steve Allen (Dr Herman Schlick), Christopher Robert Morley (Timmy Arden), Alexandra Heilweil (Miss Arden).

The Story: A woman is shipwrecked on a desert island for five years. She returns to her home on the day her husband is about to marry someone else.

Behind The Scenes: Marilyn lost 15lbs in the run up to filming and looked absolutely terrific for her costume tests on 10 April 1962. The next day she was found in a barbiturate coma by producer Weinstein. Marilyn often reported sick during filming. On 19 May 1962 she appeared at President John F Kennedy's 45th birthday party. On 8 June Marilyn was fired by Fox boss Peter Levathes. The studio tried to hire another actress and settled on Lee Remick. However, Dean Martin who had co-star approval refused to work with her much to Marilyn's absolute joy. "I have the greatest respect for Miss Remick and her talent and for all other actresses who were considered for the rôle, but I signed to do the picture with Marilyn Monroe, and I will do it with no one else." On 1 August, three days before she passed away, Marilyn resigned to make the film.

Did You Know?: The film was a remake of the 1940 Cary Grant movie *My Favorite Wife*. The original script by Samuel and Bella Spewack was inspired by a poem written by Alfred, Lord Tennyson. Marilyn was paid a third of the money given to director Cukor and co-star Martin.

6. Marilyn's Death

Marilyn was buried in Westwood Village Memorial Park, 1218 Glendon Avenue, Los Angeles 90024. Marilyn's death has been the subject of enormous speculation for many years and there seems to be no likelihood of it stopping in the near future. Was she murdered? Did she commit suicide? Did she die accidentally? Accounts vary according to who is talking. What is known is that according to the autopsy and death certificate Marilyn died of 'acute barbiturate poisoning due to ingestion of overdose.' Among the many unanswered questions about her death was how Marilyn managed to swallow up to 40 Nembutals without a glass being in her room and anyway the water had been turned off at the mains during decoration.

The Theories

• **The Attorney-General did it...** According to biographer Donald Wolfe, Marilyn spent her last afternoon at her home, 12305 Fifth Helena Drive, Brentwood, in the presence of her PR Pat Newcomb and her housekeeper Eunice Murray plus her son-in-law Norman Jefferies. Marilyn and Newcomb had a fight and the PR was asked to leave. That afternoon at around 3.30pm Attorney General Bobby Kennedy arrived at the house with Peter Lawford and the actor told Murray and Jefferies to go to the market. They were gone for about an hour. Later between 9.30 and 10pm Kennedy returned with two men and ordered Murray and Jefferies out of the house. When they went back in they found a naked Marilyn lying in a comatose state in the guest cottage, not the master bedroom. An ambulance was called but Marilyn died on the way to the hospital and was returned to her house, placed in bed and the cover-up began.

• **The Attorney-General and the Brother-In-Law did it...** According to Marilyn's long-time friend Jim Haspiel, Bobby Kennedy and Peter Lawford told Marilyn to stop calling JFK. In a fit of temper RFK smothered Marilyn with a pillow and then ordered Lawford to make it appear like a suicide. After RFK left Lawford discovered Marilyn was still alive but she died on the way to hospital in an ambulance and the suicide cover-up was put into place.

- **The Housekeeper and the Doctor did it…** Yet another biographer Donald Spoto claims that Eunice Murray and Dr Ralph Greenson killed Marilyn by administering a barbiturate enema.
- **The Doctor did it…** Ambulance driver James Hall claims that he was called to Marilyn's house on the night she died and, with his partner, began to administer CPR when Dr Ralph Greenson killed Marilyn by administering a hypodermic needle under her breast.
- **The CIA did it…** One theory has it that the CIA murdered Marilyn to prevent scandal engulfing the White House. This theory doesn't take into account the facts that every White House correspondent knew about Kennedy's womanising and the CIA were no great fans of JFK.
- **The Mafia did it…** In a biography of Mafioso Sam 'Momo' Giancana, the Mafia apparently made Marilyn a star through its association with Joseph Schenck and Harry Cohn. They also put John Kennedy in the White House through their association with Joseph Kennedy. JFK then sent secret FBI documents to Giancana using Marilyn and actress Angie Dickinson as couriers. When FBI chief J Edgar Hoover discovered what was happening he ordered JFK to cut his links with the mob. In a bid to get back at the President, Giancana ordered Marilyn's execution.
- **Fidel Castro did it…** Writer Tony Scaduto claims that Castro had Marilyn bumped off either as revenge for the CIA's bungled attempts on his own life or in retaliation for the Bay of Pigs.
- **Marilyn did it…** Biographers Fred Lawrence Guiles, Roger Kahn and Barbara Leaming postulate the suicide theory.
- **Marilyn did it accidentally…** According to writer Hank Messick, Marilyn set out to embarrass Bobby Kennedy by pretending to commit suicide but was rather too adept for her own good.
- **Aliens did it…** Probably the most far-fetched theory comes from writer Robert Slatzer and private detective Milo Speriglio who claimed, in 1996, that Marilyn was killed because she knew the truth about the 1947 Roswell Incident and was about to reveal all!
- **No one did it…** On 21 June 1983 the American tabloid *The National Examiner* ran a story claiming that Marilyn hadn't died after all but had been confined to a lunatic asylum by government agents for 21 years. Ho-hum. You pays your money…

7. The Best & Worst Films

Some time ago, I polled leading film critics on both sides of the Atlantic to discover what, in their opinions, were Marilyn's 3 Best and 3 Worst films. The results, published for the first time, are as follows:

The Best
1. *Some Like It Hot*
2. *The Seven Year Itch*
3. *Bus Stop*
4. *The Misfits*
5. *Gentlemen Prefer Blondes*
6. *How To Marry A Millionaire*
7. *Niagara*
8. *The Asphalt Jungle*
9. *All About Eve*

The Worst
1. *The Prince & The Showgirl*
2. *Let's Make Love*
3. *Niagara*
4. *River Of No Return*
5. *There's No Business Like Showbusiness*
=6. *Don't Bother To Knock*
=6. *Love Happy*
8. *As Young As You Feel*
=9. *Gentlemen Prefer Blondes*
=9. *Monkey Business*

8. The 16 Directors Marilyn Agreed To Work With

Under the terms of her new contract with Fox in 1955 Marilyn was given directorial approval. She chose 16 directors with whom she would agree to work. They were as follows:

George Stevens (1904-1975) He never got the opportunity to work with Marilyn although Stevens did direct another potent 20th century sex symbol James Dean in *Giant* (1956).

Fred Zinneman (1907-1997) Zinnemann directed *High Noon* (1952), which won four Oscars and saw Zinnemann nominated, and *From Here To Eternity* (1953), which won eight Oscars including Best Director for Zinnemann. He won Oscars for Best Film and Best Director on *A Man For All Seasons* (1966). He was also nominated for *The Nun's Story* (1958), *The Sundowners* (1960) and *Julia* (1977). He wrote an article on directing for the *Encyclopædia Britannica*. Hating Hollywood, Zinnemann moved to London permanently in 1963. Towards the end of his career he was summoned by a young executive at a film studio who began the meeting with "Tell me about a few things that you've done." Zinnemann responded dryly: "You first."

Billy Wilder (1906-) Wilder directed Marilyn in *The Seven Year Itch* and *Some Like It Hot*.

Willie Wyler (1902-1981) Wyler was a business student who didn't even consider a career in films until he was asked to visit the States by his relative Carl Laemmle. He began working at Universal as a publicist before moving behind the camera to become a highly successful director winning Oscars for *Mrs Miniver* (1942), *The Best Years Of Our Lives* (1946) and *Ben Hur* (1959). In 1965 he was awarded the Irving G Thalberg Award for lifetime achievement. Ten of his films earned Best Film nominations.

Alfred Hitchcock (1899-1980) Hitchcock never worked with Marilyn. Hitchcock was the master of the suspense thriller. He found great satisfaction in carefully planning each film and thought the actual execution to be a bore. His famous comment "Actors should be treated like cattle" only meant that they were there to bring to life his vision and for no other reason. Among the films he directed are *The 39 Steps* (1935), *Rebecca* (1940), *Rear Window* (1954), *To Catch A Thief* (1955), *North By Northwest* (1959), *The Birds* (1963), *Marnie* (1964), and *Frenzy* (1971). His most famous is probably *Psycho* (1960), the story of the mother-fixated Norman Bates, proprietor of the Bates Motel. The devoutly Catholic Hitchcock donated £20,000 for a chapel to be built at the Jesuit school of the present author. The gift was kept a secret until after his death.

Vittorio DeSica (1901-1974) DeSica won four Oscars for Best Foreign Film but never worked with Monroe.

Joe Mankiewicz (1909-1993) Joseph Leo Mankiewicz began as a journalist and joined Famous Players-Lasky-Paramount where he worked on many films before moving to M-G-M where he became a producer. Moving to 20th Century-Fox he began to direct. "because I couldn't stomach what was being done with what I wrote." His body of work includes *A Letter To Three Wives* (1949) for which he won Oscars as Best Director and Best Screenplay, *House Of Strangers* (1949), *No Way Out* (1950) for which he was nominated for an Oscar, *All About Eve* (1950) probably his best film and certainly the one that showed his talent for bitchy dialogue and for which he again won Oscars as Best Director and Best Screenplay, *Julius Cæsar* (1953), *Guys And Dolls* (1955), *Cleopatra* (1963) and *Sleuth* (1972).

George Cukor (1899-1983) Cukor directed Marilyn in *Let's Make Love* ("You never really know about chemistry. I directed Monroe and Montand in *Let's Make Love* which they proceeded to do. Miss Signoret was accompanying her husband, but right under her nose he had an affair with Marilyn. They were intoxicated with each other. But on the screen? Marilyn. Yves. Nothing!") and was also the director of her last unfinished film. After directing on Broadway in the 1920s, Cukor directed Katharine Hepburn in her first film A *Bill Of Divorcement* (1932). They would work together ten times. He began directing some memorable films including *Dinner At Eight* (1933), *Little Women* (1933), *David Copperfield* (1935), *Sylvia Scarlett* (1936), *The Prisoner Of Zenda* (1937) and began work on *Gone With The Wind* (1939) on 26 January 1939. He was sacked on 12 February. There have been any number of theories to explain the firing. Cukor was a middle-class, Jewish (very closeted) homosexual (John Carradine recalled, "He was the type of gay Jew who would never dream of admitting to anyone that, yes, he was gay and he was Jewish. Above all he wished to be thought very rich yet very common…"). In his younger days Clark Gable had serviced Billy Haines, a friend of Cukor. Haines would have told Cukor and this made Gable unhappy at the knowledge the director knew of his gay past. Cukor constantly called Gable "Dear" or "Darling" on set which he did to everyone male and female. Did Gable see this as an unsubtle dig at his masculinity? Gable claimed, "Fuck this! I won't be directed by a fairy – I have to work with a real man." Gable believed that Cukor would favour Vivien Leigh. Producer David O Selznick didn't believe Cukor good enough. His dismissal rankled with Cukor for the rest of his long life although he churned out notable fare such as *The Philadelphia Story* (1940), *Gaslight* (1944), *Adam's Rib* (1949), *A Star Is Born* (1954), *Lust For Life* (1956) and *My Fair Lady* (1964) which won him his only Oscar.

Elia Kazan (1909-) Controversial director because he named names during the McCarthy era. He never worked with Marilyn.

Carol Reed (1906-1976) Reed directed *Odd Man Out* (1947), *The Fallen Idol* (1948) and *The Third Man* (1949). His most commercially successful feature came towards the end of the 1960s. *Oliver!* (1968) won Reed an Oscar for Best Director and picked up four other gongs including Best Picture and four other nominations. It also co-starred his rambunctious nephew, Oliver.

David Lean (1908-1991) Lean who never worked with Marilyn was the son of devout Quakers who heartily disapproved of his passion for what they regarded as 'sinful' films. Celebrated director of *Brief Encounter* (1945), *The Bridge On The River Kwai* (1957), *Lawrence Of Arabia* (1962), *Doctor Zhivago* (1965), *Ryan's Daughter* (1970) and *A Passage To India* (1984). Lean was Oscar-nominated for writing, directing and editing. He so loved film-making he once quipped, only half-jokingly, "I hope the money men don't find out that I'd pay them to let me do this."

John Huston (1906-1987) Huston directed Marilyn in *The Asphalt Jungle* and *The Misfits*. He also directed *The Maltese Falcon* (1941), *The Treasure Of The Sierra Madre* (1948), *Key Largo* (1948), *The Red Badge Of Courage* (1951), *The African Queen* (1951), *Moulin Rouge* (1952), *Beat The Devil* (1954), *Moby Dick* (1956), *Casino Royale* (1967), *The Man Who Would Be King* (1975) among others. On 25 September 1933 Huston ran over and killed a pedestrian on Sunset Boulevard. M-G-M chief Louis B Mayer paid out $400,000 to hush up the incident and Huston left for England for an indefinite period.

Joshua Logan (1908-1988) Joshua Lockwood Logan III preferred the stage but loved the cinema. He worked on *Picnic* (1955) and *Mister Roberts* (1955) before being assigned to direct Marilyn in *Bus Stop* (1956). He rated Marilyn highly: "When I tell people Marilyn

81

Monroe may be one of the finest dramatic talents of our time, they laugh in my face. But I believe it. I believe it to such an extent that I would like to direct her in every picture she wants me for, every story she can dig up." Marilyn received the best reviews in her career for the film and Logan is one of the few directors who never criticised the star. "Monroe is as near genius as any actress I ever knew… She is the most completely realised actress since Garbo. Watch her work. In any film. How rarely she has to use words. How much she does with her eyes, her lips, with slight, almost accidental gestures… Monroe is pure cinema." Next Logan worked on *South Pacific* (1958), *Camelot* (1967) and Lerner & Loewe's musical *Paint Your Wagon* (1969).

Vincente Minnelli (1903-1986) The grandson of an Italian revolutionary, Minnelli was shy, unattractive, effeminate, cosmetic-wearing, inarticulate, beset by a tic and homosexual. He had directed a number of stage shows and three films when he was flung into the big time and given the chance to direct Judy Garland in *Meet Me In St Louis* (1944). Garland was often late or didn't bother to show up at all. She was reliant on drugs and had just finished an affair with Joseph L Mankiewicz and on the rebound took up with her leading man Tom Drake. Unfortunately, Drake was gay but Judy took his inability to get an erection as a personal insult. With all these distractions the film could have been a disaster. It was thanks to Minnelli's skill that it wasn't. The *Los Angeles Times* lauded it as 'one of the Great American Family sketches' and the movie became a box-office smash. It was against this background that Garland fell in love with Vincente Minnelli. He had made her look stunning on film. Not long after the film wrapped they began living together, Judy studiously ignoring the clues to Minnelli's true sexuality. Minnelli worked on *Yolanda And The Thief* (1945) which flopped, *The Clock* (1945) and *Ziegfeld Follies* (1946) the last two which teamed him once again, professionally, with Garland. They married on 15 June 1945 in Judy's mother's house and M-G-M chief Louis B Mayer gave the bride away. Minnelli next directed Judy in *The Pirate* (1948), a film about mistaken identities. Judy was out of her head on pills during most of the filming, missing 99 of the 135-day schedule. The drugs caused paranoia, the paranoia was addressed to her husband and the film was a financial flop. As they approached their second wedding anniversary, the strains were beginning to tell. She had him replaced on *Easter Parade* (1948) much to his disappointment and embarrassment. He directed *Madame Bovary*

(1949) and *Father Of The Bride* (1950) and on 21 December 1950 the couple announced their marriage was at an end. Without the heartache of Judy Garland, Minnelli seemed to thrive and directed highly successful musicals for M-G-M. His films, which garnered 20 Oscars, included: *Father's Little Dividend* (1951), *An American In Paris* (1951), *The Band Wagon* (1953), *Kismet* (1955), *Lust For Life* (1956), *Gigi* (1958), *The Sandpiper* (1965) and *On A Clear Day You Can See Forever* (1970).

Lee Strasberg (1901-1982) Strasberg's reputation has become polarised. He is either demonised or worshipped. From 1948 he ran the infamous Actors' Studio in New York and numbered some of Hollywood's greats under his patronage: Marlon Brando, Montgomery Clift, Robert De Niro, James Dean, Sally Field, Jane Fonda, Julie Harris, Steve McQueen, Paul Newman, Al Pacino, Geraldine Page, Maureen Stapleton and Rod Steiger. The Method required actors to dredge up personal feelings in order to play a rôle. Some believed in it wholeheartedly, others like Laurence Olivier dismissed it. Strasberg once opined that he had taught two great acting talents: Marilyn Monroe and Brando. When Marilyn married Arthur Miller it was Strasberg who gave the bride away. Six years later, he delivered the eulogy at her funeral. He turned to acting in later life appearing in *The Godfather: Part II* (1974) as Hyman Roth for which he was nominated for a Best Supporting Actor Oscar.

John Ford (1895-1973) One-eyed Ford never worked with Marilyn. He was the youngest of thirteen children. His father was a publican and young John joined his elder brother in show business before making his name (adopted in 1923) as the foremost director of westerns. He helped the careers of numerous actors including John Wayne and Henry Fonda despite his low opinion of the profession. "Actors are crap" he once said. Ford also said, "Anybody can direct a picture once they know the fundamentals. Directing is not a mystery, it's not an art. The main thing about directing is: photograph the people's eyes."

9. Where Are They Now?

What happened to some of the principals in Marilyn's life following her death?

Gladys Baker

Marilyn's mother. Born in Ciudad Porfirio Diaz, Mexico, at 4.30am on 27 May 1902, Gladys Pearl Monroe was the daughter of a mentally unstable family. She married for the first time on 17 May 1917 to the mysterious Jasper Newton Baker aka Jack Baker. They had two children before divorcing on 11 May 1923. On 11 October 1924 she married Martin Edward Mortenson who did a runner when Gladys became pregnant. She would spend much of the rest of her life in and out of various hospitals and sanatoriums. On 14 April 1949 she married John Stewart Eley. He died of heart disease on 23 April 1952. In 1967 Gladys was placed under the legal guardianship of her daughter Berniece. She died in Collins Court, an old folks home located at 4201 South West Twenty-First Place, Gainesville, Florida, of heart failure on 11 March 1984. She was 81 years old.

Joe DiMaggio

Marilyn's second husband. Born in Martinez, California, on 25 November 1914, DiMaggio married his first wife, blonde actress Dorothy Arnold (b. Duluth, Minnesota, 21 November 1917 as Dorothy Arnoldine Olsen d. Palm Springs, California, 13 November 1984), on 19 November 1939. They had one son, Joe Jr, born on 23 October 1941. They divorced in Reno in 1944. DiMaggio was a quiet, introspective, occasionally violent man who jealously guarded his and Marilyn's privacy. He would resort to using his fists during an argument. (Marilyn can be seen sporting a bruise courtesy of Joe when she announced her separation from DiMaggio.) He hated Hollywood and all it stood for. Following Marilyn's death DiMaggio never spoke publicly of her. He would willingly talk about baseball to fans but the shutters went up immediately when Marilyn's name was mentioned. DiMaggio died aged 84 on 8 March 1999 shortly after an operation for lung cancer. His son, from whom he was estranged due to Joe Jr's continued closeness to Marilyn after Joe Sr fell out with her, died from natural causes aged 57, five months later on 6 August 1999.

Jim Dougherty

Marilyn's first husband. Born on 12 April 1921, following his divorce from Norma Jeane, he married Patricia Scoman in 1947. He became a policeman. They had three daughters before their 1972 divorce. He married for a third time to Rita in the 1970s. He lives in Maine.

Hyman Engelberg

Marilyn's doctor. Engelberg was recommended to Marilyn by Ralph Greenson. Between 29 June and 3 August 1962 Marilyn saw Engelberg 29 times. According to his records he gave her a number of injections on 1 and 3 August yet when Dr Thomas Noguchi performed Marilyn's autopsy none of these needle marks could be found. It was Engelberg who pronounced Marilyn dead and rang the police to inform them.

'Doc' Goddard

Marilyn's honorary 'Daddy.' He was born in Holland, Texas, in 1905 and had three children when he married Grace McKee. He was killed in a car crash in Los Angeles on 4 December 1972.

Milton Greene

Marilyn's business partner. When they met Marilyn, surprised at his youthful looks, supposedly said: "Why, you're just a boy!" to which he responded "And you're just a girl." Nonetheless, it was with Milton Hawthorne Greene that she set up Marilyn Monroe Productions, Inc on 31 December 1954. Their first and only project was *The Prince & The Showgirl*. The partnership ended in April 1957. Greene was bisexual and one day his wife seduced his gay lover on the back seat of a car while Greene met with Marilyn in her suite at the Waldorf Towers. Greene died of cancer on 5 August 1985. He was 63.

Dr Ralph Greenson

Marilyn's psychiatrist. Romeo Samuel Greenschpoon was born in Brooklyn, New York, on 20 September 1911, a twin (his sister is called, what else?, Juliet), and met Marilyn in 1960 through her lawyer Mickey Rudin (Greenson's brother-in-law). From 1961, when Marilyn moved to Los Angeles, she saw Greenson three times day at his home. He also introduced her to his family which is strictly unethical behaviour for a psychiatrist. She spent her last Christmas Day at the Greensons'. As with many others in Marilyn's life all sorts of actions including murder and motives have been ascribed to Greenson. The psychiatrist remained silent in the face of all these accusations. Following Donald Spoto's book in which he accused Greenson and Eunice Murray of killing Marilyn, former deputy district attorney John Miner approached Greenson's widow and asked if he might be allowed to break the promise of confidentiality he gave Greenson during an interview with him on 12 August 1962 after Marilyn's death. Then Greenson played tapes made by Marilyn in which she spoke explicitly of sexual relationships with both Kennedys and her plans for the future. It was Greenson's conclusion that Marilyn had not committed suicide. Greenson died of heart failure on 24 November 1979. His doctor? Dr Hyman Engelberg.

John F Kennedy

Marilyn's lover. The 35th and youngest and only Roman Catholic President of America, John Fitzgerald Kennedy was born in Brookline, Massachusetts, on 29 May 1917. Numerous rumours and factoids have surfaced about Marilyn's relationship with Kennedy. One source has him fathering a child by her in 1947, another that their relationship began in the 1950s while he was still a Senator, a third that they had a one-night stand and a fourth that Kennedy took part in orgies with her including one at the Carlyle Hotel following his 45th birthday party in May 1962. As we have seen there is a very reliable eyewitness who states categorically that rather than being in bed with the President, Marilyn was in her own apartment at 4am following the bash. Kennedy was assassinated in Dallas, Texas, on 22 November 1963. Possibly the most ludicrous assertion about Monroe and Kennedy was made by 'best-selling author' Allan Silverman in a book published in 2000. He claims that in early 1939 Norma Jeane had an affair with a man called Jack Harvey and became pregnant by him. Their son was born on 18 October 1939, at which time Norma Jeane was a few months past her 13th birthday. That son was adopted and grew up to be Lee Harvey Oswald. It was in revenge for the way the Kennedys treated his mother, Marilyn Monroe, that Oswald assassinated the President!!

Robert F Kennedy

Marilyn's lover. Born in New York on 20 November 1925, Bobby Kennedy was Attorney-General in his brother's administration. Like his brother the facts regarding his relationship with Marilyn are sketchy. Some say they began a relationship in 1961 while others state that the two met for the first time on 1 February 1962 when JFK sent his brother to warn off Marilyn and rather than doing that fell in love with her himself. Biographer Donald Spoto asserts that the two never had an affair at all. Writer Bob Slatzer says Marilyn confided in him that RFK had promised to leave his wife Ethel and marry her. Both brothers apparently told Marilyn important state secrets during pillow talk. Following his brother's death Bobby resigned from the Justice Department and became Senator for New York. In June 1968 while campaigning for the Presidency he was assassinated in the kitchen of the Ambassador's Hotel, Los Angeles, where Marilyn's first modelling agency had been based.

Natasha Lytess

Marilyn's drama coach. A head of drama at Columbia Studios, Viennese-born (in 1903 as Liesl Massary) Jewish Natasha was appointed Marilyn's coach in April 1948. She worked with the actress for the next seven years until the end of *The Seven Year Itch* after which she was summarily sacked by telegram. She died of cancer in Switzerland in 1964.

Arthur Miller

Marilyn's husband. Born on 17 October 1915, Marilyn's final husband found love on the set *of The Misfits* with Magnum photographer Inge Morath (b. 1922). They married on 7 February 1962 and their daughter, Rebecca, was born on 15 September 1962. Miller wrote the play *After The Fall* (1964) which is presumed by many to be based on Marilyn although Miller denies this. He is right - it is based on Norma Jeane Mortenson. Miller lives with his wife in Connecticut and published his autobiography, *Timebends*, in 1987.

Yves Montand

Marilyn's lover. Montand was seen as a great French lover when, in fact, he wasn't French at all. He was born, after a 13-hour labour, in Monsummano Alto, Tuscany, Italy, the son of Jewish peasants, on 13 October 1921. Montand became a music-hall star of the Moulin Rouge when he was 19 thanks to the interest shown in his talent by Edith Piaf. On 14 August 1949 he met and, supposedly, fell in love with Simone Signoret and they married on 22 December 1951. She introduced him to extreme left-wing politics (he didn't renounce communism until 1968). Meanwhile, Montand's star rose in France and in 1960 he set off to conquer Hollywood. He made a few films in Tinseltown before returning to France where he began to take an active rôle in politics. Montand died in Senlis, France, from a heart attack, on 9 November 1991. He was 70.

Eunice Murray

Marilyn's housekeeper. Yet another controversial figure in Marilyn's life. Eunice Joerndt was born in Chicago on 2 February (some sources give 3 March) 1902. On 12 March 1924 she married John Murray. In 1948 she sold her home at 802 Franklin Street, Santa Monica, to Dr Ralph Greenson. In late 1962, he hired her as a housekeeper-factotum for Marilyn at an initial salary of $60-per-week, later rising to $200. Marilyn didn't altogether trust Mrs Murray. It was Mrs Murray who found Marilyn dead or dying or it wasn't. Her story changed with stunning regularity. In 1985 she admitted to Anthony Summers after years of denying the fact that Bobby Kennedy had visited Marilyn on the afternoon of 4 August 1962. She later retracted this statement.

Ralph Roberts

Marilyn's masseur. Ralph Roberts was born in Salisbury, North Carolina, on 17 August 1922 and met Marilyn in 1955 through the Lee Strasbergs. They became firm friends until her death seven years later. He began working as a masseur in between acting jobs but found it so rewarding he spent much of his time tending to aching limbs rather than learning lines. 6'4" Roberts called Marilyn on 4 August 1962 to confirm dinner but the telephone was answered by Dr Ralph Greenson who told Roberts that the actress was out. Later that night Roberts' answering service received a call from a spaced-out woman. He died in March 1999.

Frank Sinatra

Marilyn's lover. Born in Hoboken, New Jersey, on 12 December 1915, in later years Sinatra became famous for his numerous come-backs. He was a friend of Joe DiMaggio and took part in the infamous 'Wrong Door Raid' with the baseball idol that landed Sinatra in court in February 1957. The two men later had a serious falling out. Sinatra was married four times. Throughout his life he was plagued by accusations of links to organised crime due, in no small part, to his links to organised crime. He died on 14 May 1998.

Robert F Slatzer

Marilyn's what? Opinions are sharply divided on Robert Slatzer. He is either a much-maligned individual who knew Marilyn intimately and married her (Anthony Summers, Donald Wolfe) or he is the biggest charlatan and fraud to walk God's earth (Donald Spoto). Slatzer was born on 4 April 1927 in Marion, Ohio, and has worked in various fields of the media including novelist (15 books to his credit), biographer (including among others John Wayne, Bing Crosby and Thelma Todd), journalist, producer and director in films and television. Slatzer told this author that he first met Marilyn briefly in 1945 before their first 'proper' meeting on 17 July 1946 in the lobby of 20th Century-Fox. They dated and lived together on and off before Slatzer claims they went down to Tijuana, Mexico, for the weekend of 3-5 October 1952. They were married on 4 October 1952 but when they returned to Hollywood they were told in no uncertain terms by Darryl F Zanuck to annul the wedding. They returned to Mexico and persuaded a lawyer to burn the marriage certificate. In 1972 Slatzer met journalist Will Fowler and told him that Marilyn's death was the result of a political conspiracy. Slatzer wanted Fowler's help into turning his work into a book. Fowler was unimpressed by Slatzer: "I said to him: 'Too bad you weren't married to Monroe. That would really make a good book.' After I had gotten into the first draft, Slatzer mentioned that he had been married to Marilyn, but 'only for a weekend.'" Fowler became suspicious and asked for his name to be taken off the book. The book was published under the title *The Life & Curious Death Of Marilyn Monroe* in 1974. Fowler adds: "Take this from the one who removed his name from the book: Robert Slatzer was never married to Marilyn Monroe. He met the star only once. That was in Niagara Falls, New York, where he had his only pictures taken with her while she was making the movie, *Niagara*... Slatzer never met Marilyn before or since that time." During research for his biography of Marilyn, Donald Spoto discovered a cheque written by Marilyn on 4 October 1952 for $313.13 payable to Jax, a shop on Wilshire Boulevard. Marilyn had bought various garments and accessories. Underneath her signature she listed her current address: 2393 Castilian Drive, Outpost Estates, Hollywood Hills. However, journalist Dorothy Kilgallen reported in her column on 16 August 1952: 'A dark horse in the MM romance derby is Bob Slatzer, former Columbus, Ohio, literary critic. He's been wooing her by phone and mail, improving her mind with gifts of the world's greatest books.' Yet Slatzer did, by his own admission, occasionally ghost a column for Kilgallen. Is it possible he wrote this filler himself? Author George Carpozi who rewrote Slatzer's first biography of Marilyn and doesn't believe he was ever married to Marilyn writes of Slatzer and Marilyn's friendship in his own book in 1961, *eleven years* before Slatzer approached Will Fowler. Whatever the extent of Slatzer's relationship with Marilyn in life, he has certainly worked hard to keep her name alive and investigate the causes of her death. Following two failed marriages Slatzer lives in Hollywood with his wife, Debbie.

Whitey Snyder

Marilyn's make-up artist. Allan Snyder did Marilyn's make-up at her screen test on 19 July 1946 and also prepared her for her funeral on 7 August 1962. During the filming of *Gentlemen Prefer Blondes* Marilyn said: "Will you promise me that if something happens to me in this world, when I die or anything like that, promise me you'll do my make-up, so I look good when I leave." Jokingly, he said: "Sure, bring the body back while it's warm." She sent him a 14-carat gold money clip with the words "Whitey Dear: While I'm still warm. Marilyn." When Marilyn died, Joe DiMaggio rang him and said "Whitey, you promised." Snyder kept his promise but had to drink almost a bottle of gin to do so. He was the father-in-law of Kim Basinger.

Lee Strasberg

Marilyn's drama coach and preferred director.

Paula Strasberg

Marilyn's drama coach. Paula Miller (b. 1911) replaced Natasha Lytess as Marilyn's drama coach from *Bus Stop* onwards. In general Paula has received a bad press from Marilyn biographers but, in reality, she was devoted to her pupil and was often used to prevent unwanted people getting through to Marilyn. John Huston remarked on the set of *The Misfits*: "I think we're doing Paula a disservice. For all we know she's been holding this picture together." She died of cancer in 1966.

Darryl F Zanuck

Marilyn's enemy. Darryl Francis Zanuck was born on 5 September 1902 on the second floor of Le Grande Hotel, an establishment managed by his father on the corner of Fifth Street and Broadway in Wahoo, Nebraska. He began his career writing pulp fiction but realised that the real money was made by the screenwriters who adapted works for the cinema. He became a joke writer for, among others, Mack Sennett, Harold Lloyd and Charlie Chaplin. Like many in Hollywood Zanuck was short – just 5'5". He was one of the founders of 20th Century-Fox and had a love-hate relationship with Marilyn from the time she signed with the studio on 26 August 1946. Zanuck simply never rated Marilyn as an actress despite the urgings of his subordinates and other moguls. He would stride around the Fox lot wearing riding boots and jodhpurs carrying a crop which he would beat against his leg or on a desk to make a point. Zanuck insisted that none of his male stars have hairy chests. The bald-chested Tyrone Power was okay but hirsute hunks like William Holden had to shave their chests. He demanded that one of the Fox actresses had sex with him in his office every afternoon. He would often flash his penis at actresses. Once he took it out before Betty Grable and put it on the desk. "Isn't it beautiful?" he asked. "Yes," she said, "and you can put it away now." Zanuck was summoned back to 20th Century-Fox to try and rescue the company from the financial mire that the film *Cleopatra* (1963) had landed them in. Displacing Spyros Skouras on 25 July, he became President of the company appointing his son, Richard, as Vice President with responsibility for production. On 28 August 1969 Richard became President while Darryl took over as Chairman and CEO. The following year, on 29 December 1970, he sacked his son and consolidated his position, but only until 18 May 1971 when he became Chairman Emeritus. Zanuck suffered an inoperable brain tumour that left him incoherent and spent his last days in paranoid seclusion in Palm Springs. He died on 22 December 1979.

10. Bibliography

This is a short list of just some of the books of Monrovia.

The Agony Of Marilyn Monroe – George Carpozi, Jr (London: Consul Books, 1962)

The Assassination Of Marilyn Monroe – Donald H Wolfe (London: Little, Brown, 1998)

The Birth Of Marilyn The Lost Photographs Of Norma Jeane By Joseph Jasgur – Jeannie Sakol (London: Sidgwick & Jackson, 1991)

The Complete Films Of Marilyn Monroe – Mark Ricci & Michael Conway (Secausus: Citadel Press, 1964)

Conversations With Marilyn – W J Weatherby (London: Sphere, 1987)

Crypt 33 The Saga Of Marilyn Monroe – The Final Word – Adela Gregory & Milo Speriglio (New York: Birch Lane Press, 1993)

Falling For Marilyn The Lost Niagara Collection – Jock Carroll (London: Virgin, 1996)

Finding Marilyn A Romance – David Conover (New York: Grossett & Dunlap, 1981)

Goddess The Secret Lives Of Marilyn Monroe – Anthony B Summers (London: Victor Gollancz, 1985)

Joe And Marilyn A Memory Of Love – Roger Kahn (London: Sidgwick & Jackson, 1987)

The Last Sitting – Bert Stern (London: Black Cat, 1982)

The Life And Curious Death Of Marilyn Monroe – Robert F Slatzer (New York: Pinnacle Books, 1982)

The Making Of The Misfits – James Goode (New York: Limelight Editions, 1986)

Marilyn – Joe Hembus (London: Tandem, 1973)

Marilyn – Gloria Steinem & George Barris (London: Victor Gollancz, 1987)

Marilyn – Neil Sinyard (Leicester: Magna Books, 1989)

The Marilyn Files – Robert F Slatzer (New York: SPI, 1992)

Marilyn Lives! – Joel Oppenheimer (London: Pipeline Books, 1981)

Marilyn Monroe – Maurice Zolotow (London: W H Allen, 1961)

Marilyn Monroe – Joan Mellen (London: Star Books, 1975)

Marilyn Monroe – Janice Anderson (London: W H Smith, 1983)

Marilyn Monroe – Graham McCann (Cambridge: Polity Press, 1988)

Marilyn Monroe – Barbara Leaming (London: Weidenfeld & Nicolson, 1998)

Marilyn A Biography – Norman Mailer (London: Spring Books, 1988)

Marilyn A Hollywood Life – Ann Lloyd (London: W H Smith, 1989)

Marilyn And Me – Susan Strasberg (London: Doubleday, 1992)

Marilyn Monroe And The Camera – Lothar Schirmer (London: Bloomsbury, 1989)

Marilyn Monroe A Life Of The Actress – Carl E Rollyson, Jr (Ann Arbor: UMI Research Press, 1986)

Marilyn Monroe A Life On Film – David Robinson & John Kobal (London: Hamlyn, 1974)

Marilyn Monroe A Never-Ending Dream – Guus Luijters (London: Plexus, 1986)

Marilyn Monroe An Appreciation – Eve Arnold (London: Hamish Hamilton, 1987)

Marilyn At Twentieth Century-Fox – Lawrence Crown (London: Planet Books, 1987)

Marilyn Among Friends – Sam Shaw & Norman Rosten (London: Bloomsbury, 1987)

The Marilyn Conspiracy – Milo Speriglio with Steven Chain (London: Corgi, 1986)

Marilyn Monroe Confidential – Lena Pepitone and William Stadiem (London: Sidgwick & Jackson, 1979)

Marilyn Her Life In Her Own Words – George Barris (London: Headline, 1995)

Monroe Her Life In Pictures – James Spada with George Zeno (London: Sidgwick & Jackson, 1982)

Marilyn Monroe In Her Own Words – Guus Luijters (London: Omnibus Press, 1991)

Marilyn The Last Take – Peter Harry Brown & Patte B Barham (London: William Heinemann, 1992)

Marilyn Mon Amour – André de Dienes (London: Sidgwick & Jackson, 1986)

Marilyn Monroe: Murder Cover-Up – Milo Speriglio (Van Nuys: Seville Publishing, 1982)

Marilyn On Location – Bart Mills (London: Sidgwick & Jackson, 1989)

Marilyn On Marilyn – Roger G Taylor (London: Comet, 1983)

The Marilyn Scandal Her True Life Revealed By Those Who Knew Her – Sandra Shevey (London: Sidgwick & Jackson, 1987)

Marilyn Monroe The Biography – Donald Spoto (London: Chatto & Windus, 1993)

Marilyn The Tragic Venus – Edwin P Hoyt (London: Robert Hale, 1965)

Marilyn The Ultimate Look At The Legend – James Haspiel (London: Smith Gryphon, 1991)

Marilyn's Addresses – Michelle Finn (London: Smith Gryphon, 1995)

Marilyn's Men The Private Life Of Marilyn Monroe – Jane Ellen Wayne (London: Robson Books, 1992)

The Men Who Murdered Marilyn – Matthew Smith (London: Bloomsbury, 1996)

Milton's Marilyn – James Kotsilibas-Davis & Joshua Greene (London: Schirmer Art Books, 1994)

My Sister Marilyn A Memoir Of Marilyn Monroe – Berniece Baker Miracle & Mona Rae Miracle (London: Weidenfeld & Nicolson, 1994)

My Story – Marilyn Monroe (New York: Stein & Day, 1974)

My Week With Marilyn – Colin Clark (London: HarperCollins, 2000)

Norma Jean The Life Of Marilyn Monroe – Fred Lawrence Guiles (London: W H Allen, 1969)

Norma Jeane The Life And Death Of Marilyn Monroe – Fred Lawrence Guiles (London: Granada, 1985)

The Prince, The Showgirl And Me – Colin Clark (London: HarperCollins, 1995)

Requiem For Marilyn – Bernard of Hollywood (Bourne End: The Kensal Press, 1986)

The Ultimate Marilyn – Ernest W Cunningham (Los Angeles: Renaissance Books, 1998)

The Unabridged Marilyn Her Life From A-Z – Randall Riese & Neal Hitchens (New York: Congdon & Weed, 1987)

Who Killed Marilyn? – Tony Sciacca (New York: Manor Books, 1976)

Young Marilyn Becoming The Legend – James Haspiel (London: Smith Gryphon, 1994)

The Essential Library

Why not try other titles in the Pocket Essentials library? Each is £2.99 unless otherwise stated. Look out for new titles every month.

New This Month @ £3.99 each:

Conspiracy Theories by Robin Ramsay

Marilyn Monroe by Paul Donnelley

Also Available

Film: **Woody Allen** by Martin Fitzgerald
Jane Campion by Ellen Cheshire
Jackie Chan by Michelle Le Blanc & Colin Odell
Joel & Ethan Coen by John Ashbrook & Ellen Cheshire
David Cronenberg by John Costello (£3.99)
Film Noir by Paul Duncan
Terry Gilliam by John Ashbrook
Heroic Bloodshed edited by Martin Fitzgerald
Alfred Hitchcock by Paul Duncan
Krzysztof Kieslowski by Monika Maurer
Stanley Kubrick by Paul Duncan
David Lynch by Michelle Le Blanc & Colin Odell
Steve McQueen by Richard Luck
Brian De Palma by John Ashbrook
Sam Peckinpah by Richard Luck
Slasher Movies by Mark Whitehead (£3.99)
Vampire Films by Michelle Le Blanc & Colin Odell
Orson Welles by Martin Fitzgerald

TV: **Doctor Who** by Mark Campbell (£3.99)

Books: **Cyberpunk** by Andrew M Butler (£3.99)
Philip K Dick by Andrew M Butler (£3.99)
Noir Fiction by Paul Duncan

Available at all good bookstores, or send a cheque to: **Pocket Essentials (Dept MM), 18 Coleswood Rd, Harpenden, Herts, AL5 1EQ, UK**. Please make cheques payable to 'Oldcastle Books.' Add 50p postage & packing for each book in the UK and £1 elsewhere.

US customers can send $5.95 plus $1.95 postage & packing for each book to: **Trafalgar Square Publishing, PO Box 257, Howe Hill Road, North Pomfret, Vermont 05053, USA**. tel: 802-457-1911, fax: 802-457-1913, e-mail: tsquare@sover.net

Customers worldwide can order online at **www.pocketessentials.com**, **www.amazon.com** and at all good online bookstores.